Environment Impact Assessment

A Guide for Practices and Application

Dr.M. Vijay Prabhu

Published by

ISBN 978-93-87862-27-2
Author
Dr.M. Vijay Prabhu
Bonfring
309, 2nd Floor,
5th Street Extension, Gandhipuram,
Coimbatore-641 012.
Tamilnadu, India.
E-mail: info@bonfring.org
Website: www.bonfring.org
Phone: 0422 4213231

Preface

Environmental Impact Assessment provides students and practitioners with a clearly structured overview of the subject, as well as critical analysis and support for further studies. Written by authors with extensive research, training and practical experience in EIA (Environmental Impact Assessment), the book covers the latest EIA legislation, guidance and good practice.

Under the best of circumstances, preparing an environmental impact assessment (EIA) can be a complex and challenging task. Experience indicates that the scope and quality of such analyses varies widely throughout the world as well as internationally. Written to help practitioners and decision-makers apply best professional practices in the development of EIAs, Environmental Impact Assessment: EIA guide to provides an in depth, yet practical direction for developing a defensible analysis that meets best professional practices.

The book describes preparation of five distinct types of assessments:

- Introduction to Environment Impact Assessment (EIA)
- EIA Review and Processes
- Water Quality Assessment
- EIA Impact Analysis and Mitigation Measures in Mine Area
- Soil, Geology and Geomorphology

To date, there is significant variation and disagreement about how such analyses should be prepared. The author introduces best practices for preparing such EIAs that is intended to meet decision-making and regulatory expectations. He supplies a comprehensive and balanced skill set of tools, techniques, concepts, principles, and practices for preparing these assessments. He also includes directions for developing a comprehensive Environmental Management Systems which can be used to monitor and implement final decisions for such analyses. While the book references the many guidance is generally applicable to any international EIA process consistent with various applications.

With thorough coverage of all aspects of assessments, the book presents a theoretical introduction to the subject as well as practical guidance. It delivers state-of-the-art tools, techniques, and approaches for resolving EIA problems.

Author Profile

Dr.M. Vijay Prabhu completed his Ph.D., in Periyar University in the year of 2014 and is currently doing his Post-Doctoral Research in the same University, funded by University Grants Commission, New Delhi. He had received University Research Fellowship through Periyar University from December 2009 to August 2011 and worked as a Project Fellow in University Grants Commission Major Research Project "WATER GIS" from August 2011 to July 2014.He has been teaching and conducting research in the field of geology and environmental sciences for UG, PG level students. He has published more than 30 research papers in reputed journals National/International level. Moreover, he has a vast experience in the field of Groundwater and petroleum exploration and Environment impact assessment through Geospatial techniques. He is a fellow of the Geological Society of India. He has received Young Researcher Forum Award in the International Conference Coastal Zone Management on July 2016 which was held at Osaka, Japan.

He has contributed several invited talks and articles in magazines and newspapers. He has presented several research papers in the national and international level seminars and conferences. He has over 15 years of experience in various aspects of investigations related to groundwater exploration and environment impact assessment. He has carried out extensive hydrogeological surveys, groundwater management projects in varied hydrogeological terrains. He has a rich experience in planning and implementing groundwater development and management programmes in the hard rock terrain.

Dr.M. Vijay Prabhu's research interest includes formulating research methodology in geosciences, hydrogeology, watershed development and coastal management practices and salving environmental problems and applications. He has published several research papers in national and international journals and has authored for few editorial volumes on geology.

About this Book

As an Earth Science Teacher-cum-Post Doctoral Fellow, I believe in field based teaching in addition to classroom oriented teaching. I lead has a particular goal, and each discussion is the result of careful preparation of field oriented applications. I want them to engage in the something know about Environment Impact Assessment, I believe some concrete understanding EIA procedure and practices through this book.

I try to use important thinks easy to understand the real subject as well as words and concepts. I think that my greatest ability as a thinker, teacher, and learner is the ability to organize my thoughts. Although I try to use a wide variety of sources and applications, I take great pride in this attempt much useful to learners. What I may lack in intellectual creativity or theoretical gifts, I am planning to write of this book based on my own experience and interest in this field.

My methodological and theoretical research as well as a considerable portion of my applied and collaborative work addresses field geological data. An innovative contribution of my work is the establishment of a new perspective to the analysis. This perspective creates a new class of functional estimation procedures and correlation in an intuitive and efficient manner. This framework has produced interesting and potentially powerful results in applications. I am also involved in applied and collaborative EIA projects dealing with a wide range of data and design structures in a large number of scientific settings.

To summarize, at this point in my career, my primary interests are in hydrogeology applied to the field of watershed management and development and environment impact assessment. In the immediate future, I would like to go further advanced applications to minimize environment impact through advanced technology. In the long term I see myself working on expanding my expertise in these areas by a mixture of experimental and empirical work.

<table>
<tr><td>**Chapter**</td><td>**Contents**</td><td>**Page No**</td></tr>
</table>

Chapter	Contents	Page No
I	**Introduction to Environment Impact Assessment**	**1**
	1.1. General Introduction	1
	1.2. Objectives	1
	1.3. What is this Guide for?	2
	1.4. Important Jargon you will Need to Know	2
	1.5. So where does EIA Come from?	3
	1.6. Review for Previous Study	3
	1.7. When is an EIA required?	5
	1.8. If so, it is likely to have a Significant Effect on the Environment by Virtue of its Nature, Size or Location?	6
	1.9. Alright, so how do Local Authorities Reach a Decision on All of these Tests?	6
	1.10. Government Guidance States that EIA will be Needed for Schedule 2 Projects in Three Main Types of Cases	7
	1.11. What about Extensions to Existing Developments?	9
	1.12. Who Decides if an EIA is Required?	9
	1.13. The Local Planning Authority	9
	1.14. Identifying Alternatives	10
	1.15. What's the Format of an Environmental Statement?	12
	1.16. Non-technical Summary	13
	1.17. Environmental Statement	13
	1.18. When is an Environmental Statement not an Environmental Statement?	14
	1.19. Are the Public Entitled to See the ES and how much should it Cost?	15
	1.20. What about Assessing the Quality of EIA	15
II	**The EIA Process Overview**	**17**
	2.1. Introduction	17
	2.2. Screening	18

2.3. Purpose, Characteristics and Outcomes of Screening   18

2.4. Screening Procedures and Methods   19

2.5. Scoping   20

2.6. Roles and Objectives of Scoping   22

2.7. Methods Used in Scoping   24

2.8. EIA Terms of Reference   27

2.9. Baseline Studies   28

2.10. Project Lists for Screening   30

2.11. Extended Screening or Preliminary EIA   32

2.12. Initial Environmental Evaluation or Examination (IEE)   34

2.13. Mitigation and Impact Management   34

2.14. EIA Stage for Considering Mitigation   36

2.15. Environmental Management Plan and Mitigation Measures   37

2.16. EIA Reporting and Review   39

2.17. Executive or Non-technical Summary   41

2.18. Guidelines for Effective EIA Report Preparation and Production   44

2.19. Procedure, Steps and Methods in the EIA Review   46

2.20. EIA Review and the Acceptability of the Proposal   48

2.21. EIA Review Guideline of India   49

2.22. EIA as Part of the Decision-making Process   52

2.23. Tools for Environmental Management and Performance Review   58

2.24. Environmental Auditing   63

2.25. Evaluation of EIA Effectiveness and Performance   65

III   **Water Quality Assessment**   **67**

3.1. Introduction   67

3.2. Water Contaminants   68

3.3. Other Common Constituents of Natural Water   69

3.4. Examination of Water   71

3.5. Physical Examination of Water   73

3.6. Significance   75

3.7. Significance   76

3.8. Chemical Examination of Water   77

3.9. Significance   79

3.10. Significance   80

3.11. Bacteriological Examination of Water   82

3.12. Chemistry of Solutions   84

3.13. Water Quality Requirements   86

3.14. Potable Water Standards   87

3.15. Important Consideration in Setting National Drinking Water Quality Standards   87

IV   EIA Impact Analysis and Mitigation Measures in Mine Area   89

4.1. The Purpose of the EIA   89

4.2. Importance of EIA   89

4.3. Aim and Objectives   89

4.4. Benefits of the Study   90

4.5. Description of the Environment   90

4.6. General Approach To Environment   91

4.7. Meteorological Data   91

4.8. Air Quality Monitoring   92

4.9. Sources of Air Pollution   93

4.10. Site & Parameter Selection   94

4.11. Types of Air Quality Monitoring   94

4.12. Air Environment   96

4.13. Noise Monitoring   99

4.14. Vibration Monitoring Instruments   104

4.15. Water Monitoring   106

4.16. Climate Conditions   109

4.17. Environmental Management Plan General   110

4.18. Objective   111

4.19. Economy   111

4.20. Environmental Policy/Legislation   111

4.21. Mining Technology - Alternatives   112

4.22. Assessment of Infrastructure Demand (Physical & Social)   112

4.23. Waste & Sub-Grade Mineral Management   114

4.24. Disaster Management and Risk Assessment   115

4.25. Design of Green Belt   116

4.26. Post Plantation Care   118

4.27. Precautionary Care   119

4.28. Management Plan and Suggestion   120

V   **Soils, Geology and Geomorphology**   **121**

5.1. Introduction   121

5.2. Definitions and Concepts–Geology and Geomorphology   121

5.3. Geomorphology   122

5.4. Definitions and Concepts–Soils   122

5.5. Soil Composition   123

5.6. The Soil Profile and Soil Classification   124

5.7. Soil Structure   127

5.8. Soil Fertility   128

5.9. Land Evaluation   128

Bibliography   130

CHAPTER I

INTRODUCTION TO ENVIRONMENT IMPACT ASSESSMENT

1.1. General Introduction

Environmental Impact Assessment (EIA) is a tool for assisting environmental management and for contributing to Sustainable Development. The purpose of EIA is to identify potential environmental impacts from proposals, such as projects and programs, and to propose means to avoid or reduce the significant impacts. EIA was developed formally in the 1970s and has been incorporated in the procedures of governments and major development organizations world-wide. As a result it is important that people who may have any role in the design or planning of projects, or may be associated with deciding about their suitability, should be aware of EIA and how it operates in their local area. The Environmental Impact Assessment Course Module is designed to enable participants to gain this awareness.

The Environmental Impact Assessment has been designed to bring understanding of EIA to a wide range of students. These students may be undertaking formal studies in higher education for their first degree as undergraduate students, or doing further studies as postgraduate students. They may also be people who have been working for some time in one of the many professions where EIA has relevance: their level of formal education is likely to range from low to high. Also, while the broad principles of EIA are applicable everywhere, the details of how these principles are applied in specific countries and jurisdictions varies. As a result, the Environmental Impact Assessment Course Module has been designed to be flexible, and to be customized and made relevant to:

- Students with different educational and knowledge backgrounds;
- Students with different needs;
- Different EIA regimes around the world.

1.2. Objectives

The aims and objectives of EIA can be divided into two categories.

- To understand basic principles,Baseline data,concept and applications in water mineral and soil etc.,
- The immediate aim of EIA is to inform the process of decision making by identifying the potentially significant environmental effects and risk of development.
- The ultimate aim of EIA is to promote sustainable development by ensuring that development proposals do not undermine critical resources and ecological functions

or the well-being lifestyle and livelihood of the communities and peoples to depend on
them.

1.3.   What is this Guide for?

Environmental Impact Assessment (EIA) is a key aspect of many large scale planning
applications. It is a technique which is meant to help us understand the potential
environmental impacts of major development proposals. Unfortunately as often as not both the
process and the outcome of EIA can be complex and confusing leaving local communities
unsure as to how a development might affect them. This guide is intended as a broad
introduction to the Environmental Impact Assessment (EIA). The material is drawn from
regulations, circulars and guidance and is designed to help individuals understand what EIA is
and in what circumstances it should be applied. The guide is not intended to provide guidance
on how to prepare an EIA. For example it does not explain how to prepare an archaeological
survey or landscape assessment. The overall theme of this guide is to encourage local
communities to engage in the EIA process. Experts don't always know best and by ignoring
local knowledge their decision may have disastrous consequence for local people living near
development sites.

In a nut shell EIA is just an information gathering exercise carried out by the developer and
other bodies which enables a Local Planning Authority to understand the environmental affects
of a development before deciding whether or not it should go ahead. The really important thing
about environmental assessments is the emphasis on using the best available sources of
objective information and in carrying out a systematic and holistic process which should be
bias free and allow the local authority and the whole community to properly understand the
impact of the proposed development. Environmental assessment should lead to better
standards of development and in some cases development not happening at all. Where
developments do go ahead environmental assessments should help to propose proper
mitigation measures. Environmental impact assessment is meant to be a systematic process
which leads to a final product, the Environmental Statement (ES).

1.4.   Important Jargon you will Need to Know

- Environmental Impact Assessment (EIA) is a term used to describe the total process of
  assessing the environmental effects of a development project.
- An Environmental Statement (ES) is used to describe the written material submitted
  to the local planning authority in fulfilment of the EIA regulations.

- The term Environmental Assessment (EA) is no longer used so as to avoid confusion with the Environment Agency.

1.5. So where does EIA Come from?

The EIA process derives from European law. The European law basis is Directive 85/337, The Assessment of the Effects of Certain Public and Private Projects on the Environment as amended by EC Directive 97/11/EC. The Directive is mainly implemented in UK legislation through the Town and Country Planning (Assessment of Environmental Effects) Regulations 1999 (SI 1999 No. 293). This is generally known as the EIA Regulations. Important guidance on the interpretation of the EIA Regulations and on the procedure to be used can be found in ODPM Circular 2/99 Environmental Impact Assessment. The Regulations only cover decisions made under Town and Country Planning legislation. However, the Directive requires that all types of developments having significant impacts on the environment go through the EIA process. Therefore there are separate pieces of legislation (and some non-legislative processes) covering EIA for other types of developments including highways, power stations, water resources, land drainage, forestry, pipelines, harbour works and many others. UK regulations have been criticised as not fully interpreting the spirit of the EIA directive. Individual cases over major development proposals have led to controversial debates about quality of EIA. Third parties have complained to the European Commission about the failure of the UK Government to fully implement the EC directives on EIA. As well as the circular 2/99 there are a number of other key documents which outline the Regulations and the methodology of EIA including ODPM's Guide to Procedures: Environmental Impact Assessment.

1.6. Review for Previous Study

To know what research works have been done in this limestone field, at which point we stand in the development of the industry and from which point we have to start with, the various previous works done in this industry were reviewed. The review reveals the following contributions. Mining of economic minerals from the earths' crust has been one of the world's earliest and important human activities after agriculture (Mondal et al., 2014). Unsystematic mining activities of surface and subsurface tend to make a significant impact on the environment, resulting in reduction of forest cover, erosion of soil, pollution of air, water and land and reduction in biodiversity (Woldai, 2001; Ranade, 2007; Iqbal et al., 2013).

Geospatial data have been extensively used now for LULC mapping and environmental impact assessment and monitoring of mining activities (Rathore and Wright, 1993; Jhanwar, 1996; Charou et al., 2010). Environmental hazards related to pollution, change detection of vegetation and mining impacts can be more effectively assessed and monitored by remote sensing techniques (Stefouli and Tsombos, 1998; Woldai, 2001; Latifovic et al., 2005; Vorovencii, 2011). Therefore, remotely sensed data is widely used now in surveys and applications beyond land-use land-cover change studies due to the increased perception by researchers, professionals, Governments and Industry (Baynard, 2013). The state of Tamilnadu has vast limestone deposits with a total reserve of 1473 million tonnes (Equbal and Ambica, 2012).

Subsequently Sir Thomas Holland (1892-1900) discussed the origin of the Chalk Hills Middle Miss (1896) carried out a detailed survey of the Chalk Hills and gave some quantitative data with a map of the area. Other geologists engaged in this work in the 18th and early 19th centuries are Lacroix(1889),Davis (1909), Burlton(1912) and VineyakaRao (1929). Aiyengar (1940) gave a detailed account of limestone occurrences of Tamil Nadu in general and the Chalk Hills in particular. In these reports, he has also dealt with the classification, origin and uses of the limestone.

Crooks hank (1942), Krishnan and Aiyengar(1943) and Krishnan(1947) discussed the economic aspects of the limestone deposits. Krishnamurthy (1956- 61) described the geology of Salem limestone. The limestone occurrences of Coimbatore and Nilgris districts were first reported by Gopalakrishnan and Sankaran (1972). Srinivachari and Venkatesh identified the other areas in these districts. The limestone occurrences of the redistricts were re-examined by Bhalla (1979). Subramanian (1974) gave a list of unique occurrences of limestone in Narivalam and Vandalore areas of Trinelveli district.Srinivashari (1977 -78) visited the various minor occurrences of limestone in Tamil Nadu and on a cursory study grouped various occurrences on the basis of size and economic potentiality.

The geological Survey of India (GSI) formulated a Five year programme for reassessment of limestone deposits of Tamil Nadu (1985). On this basis, the surface geological work was carried out by the GSI in the Chalk Hills and Sirapalli area and regional drilling was under taken with a view to find out the depth persistence of ore mineralisation in the Chalk Hills area.

Mukthinath (1949), Nautiyal (1953), Agarwal and Singh (1960) studied the origin of the Himalayan limestone. They are of the opinion that the Himalayan limestone is of secondary origin formed by replacement of dolomite by magnesia rich hydrothermal solutions. These solutions are thought to have been derived from the basic intrusions in there region. Mukthinath and Wakhaloo (1962) have given a comprehensive account of the limestone occurrences in Almora district of Uttar Pradesh. Mishera and Valdiya (1961) proposed the theory of primary precipitation of the Himalayan limestone. Latter on Valdiya (1968) proposed the theory of contemporaneous placement of earlier formed carbonate assemblages.

Negi (1976) is of the view that formation of Himalayan limestone was by two processes, the digenetic replacement of pre-existing carbonate sediments as well as primary precipitation due to the favourable conditions created by algae. The GSI attached to the Government of India, conducts field experiments to trace the occurrence of limestone in the country. The Department of Mining and Geology of each State government explores the economic availability of this mineral. These works are being continuously carried out by these agencies.

1.7.   When is an EIA required?

In a simple world EIA would apply to all forms of development but just to confuse everyone EIA is required for some types of development and not others. Deciding on whether an EIA is required can be the source of major dispute between developers, communities and local authorities. The EIA regulations define two schedules of developments. For Schedule 1 projects an EIA must always be carried out. For Schedule 2 projects an EIA must be carried out if the development is likely to have a significant impact on the environment by virtue of its nature, size or location (see selection criteria below). The definitions allow for considerable uncertainty about the need for EIA in specific circumstances.

Examples of Schedule 1 projects include:

- Major power plants
- Chemical works
- Waste disposal incineration
- Major Roads Schemes

Examples of Schedule 2 Projects include:

- Quarries and opencast
- Some intensive livestock rearing
- Overhead transmission lines
- Surface storage of fossil fuel
- Foundries and forges
- Coke ovens
- Manufacture of dairy products
- Brewing
- Some textile operations
- Rubber production
- Wide range of infrastructure projects
- Waste water treatment plants

- Holiday villages

- Golf courses

- All Schedule 2 developments are based on thresholds. A proposed development only becomes a Schedule 2 development where it exceeds the threshold. For example a 'shipyard' development only falls within Schedule 2 where 'the area of new floor space exceeds 1,000 square metres' (paragraph 4.g of Schedule 2).

- It is important not to confuse the issue of 'thresholds' with the issue of whether a Schedule 2 development must undergo EIA because it is likely to have a significant effect on the environment. Just because a project falls within one of the categories set out in Schedule 2 and exceeds the Schedule 2 threshold does not mean that EIA is required. The question is still whether the proposed development is likely to have a significant effect on the environment.

The three stage process is therefore as follows:

- Is the proposed development within a category set out in Schedule 2?

- If so, either:

   a. does it exceed the threshold set out for that category in Schedule 2?

   or

   b. is it in a 'sensitive area' such as a SSSI, SPA, national park, AONB etc?

1.8. If so, it is likely to have a Significant Effect on the Environment by Virtue of its Nature, Size or Location?

- If the answer to all three of those questions is 'yes' then an EIA is required.

- If the answer to any of those questions is 'no' then an EIA is not required.

- Questions 1 and 2 are objective questions of fact. However, question 3 is a matter of opinion and different authorities may reach different views on that question. A decision on question 3 is therefore much harder to challenge in Court.

1.9. Alright, so how do Local Authorities Reach a Decision on All of these Tests?

The overall test for whether EIA is required for a Schedule 2 description of development is whether the proposed development would be likely to have significant effects on the environment by virtue of factors such as its nature, size or location.

1.10. Government Guidance States that EIA will be Needed for Schedule 2 Projects in Three Main Types of Cases

- For major projects which are of more than local importance;
- Occasionally for projects on a smaller scale which are proposed for particularly sensitive or vulnerable locations;
- In a small number of cases, for projects with unusually complex and potentially adverse environmental effects; where expert and detailed analysis of those effects would be desirable and would be relevant to the issue of principle as to whether or not the development should be permitted.

The decision should be taken by the local planning authority or the Secretary of State on a case-by-case basis taking into account the criteria set out in the new Regulations. The criteria which must be taken into account when screening a Schedule 2 development are set out in Schedule 3 to the Regulations which are as follows:

Schedule 3 selection criteria for screening schedule 2 development:

Characteristics of Development

The characteristics of development must be considered having regard, in particular, to:

- the size of the development;
- the accumulation with other development;
- the use of natural resources;
- the production of waste;
- pollution and nuisances;
- the risk of accidents, having regard in particular to substances or technologies used.

Location of Development

The environmental sensitivity of geographical areas likely to be affected by development must be considered, having regard, in particular, to:

- the existing land use
- the relative abundance, quality and regenerative capacity of natural resources in the area
- the absorption capacity of the natural environment, paying particular attention to:
  a. wetlands
  b. coastal zones
  c. mountain and forest areas

d.   nature reserves and parks

e.   areas classified or protected under Member States' legislation; areas designated by Member States pursuant to Council Directive 79/409/EEC on the conservation of wild birds[41] and Council Directive 92/43/EEC on the conservation of natural habitats and of wild fauna and flora[42]

f.   areas in which the environmental quality standards laid down in Community legislation have already been exceeded

g.   densely populated areas

h.   landscapes of historical, cultural or archaeological significance

Characteristics of the Potential Impact

The potential significant effects of development must be considered in relation to criteria set out under paragraphs 1 and 2 above, and having regard in particular to:

- The extent of the impact (geographical area and size of the affected population)
- The transfrontier nature of the impact
- The magnitude and complexity of the impact
- The probability of the impact
- The duration, frequency and reversibility of the impact.

The 1999 regulations and circular 02/99 make clear that the usual indicative criteria for requiring EIA in schedule 2 cases may not apply when the development is likely to impact on environmentally sensitive locations. Paragraph 36 of the circular makes clear that an EIA will normally be required for any development likely to have significant impacts on SSSI's and that in areas such as National Parks and areas of Outstanding Natural Beauty. The probability of requiring environmental impact assessment for particular development is increased.

There are number of complex ideas bound up in the assessment of the likely impact of the development and its consequent need for environmental impact assessment. The sensitivity of particular receptors to environmental impact may, for example includes both social and ecological impacts. Likewise there is an emerging trend to see the environmental carrying capacity of an area in terms of, not just of wildlife, but as a measure of for example air pollution and its impact on human health. This has led to an extremely important and contentious area of environmental impact assessment and planning regulation which is the assessment of health impacts and their materiality to planning decisions. For major developments Local Planning Authorities have required health impact studies to be prepared.

1.11. What about Extensions to Existing Developments?

Extensions or changes to existing development will only require environmental impact assessment if they are likely to have significant negative environmental impact. Such impact should be measured against the indicative thresholds set out in column 2 of schedule 2.

1.12. Who Decides if an EIA is Required?

A developer can decide to submit an EIA voluntarily for a large scale development. Normally, however, it is the local planning authority who decides if an EIA is required in consultation with the applicant.

1.13. The Local Planning Authority

The local planning authority may be asked informally by the applicant whether EIA is necessary for schedule 2 projects. The 1999 regulations now require a local planning authority to provide on request a formal opinion as to whether EIA should be carried out and this is termed a screening opinion. The local planning authority must be satisfied that it has received sufficient information to give a safe opinion baring in mind that the failure to require an EIA for a project subsequently found to have significant environmental impacts could be subject to costly legal challenge. The 1999 regulations require that such opinions be made public by formally recording them on the planning register.

Where an application is submitted for a development falling within any of the Schedule 2 descriptions without an ES, the local planning authority may determine that EIA is required and refuse to consider the application until an ES is submitted. Such determination should be made within three weeks, beginning with the date of receipt of the application.

The Secretary of State

The Secretary of State has reserved powers to intervene in cases where the local planning authority have failed to give an opinion on whether an EIA is needed within the prescribed period or where the applicant disagrees with the opinion given by the local planning authority.

EIA and Case Law

In recent years, there have been a large number of cases in the UK courts and the European Court of Justice that have looked at questions surrounding environmental impact assessments. One important case illustrates the range of EIA questions which the courts have dealt with: In Berkeley v Secretary of State for the Environment 2000, the House of Lords ruled that EIA could no longer be inferred. In short this means that planning authorities can no longer say that while they have not carried out an explicit EIA, their determination process amounts to an EIA by addressing key environmental impacts. This was often used as a defence by local authorities who had not required EIA. The Lords ruled that EIA was a distinct set of methods which must be applied coherently and in their entirety. In effect local authorities are now under more pressure to get their decisions about whether to require an EIA right in the first instance.

So What Stages of the EIA should we Look Out for?

1.14. Identifying Alternatives

Part II of Schedule 4 of the regulations requires the applicant to provide a reasoned decision of the main alternatives to development. These requirements raise a number of important new issues about planning decision making. It suggests for example that a developer would honestly seek to examine other development sites which may not be in their control. It also suggests that in the case of waste disposal, consideration should be given to more sustainable solutions in sectors outside the operational range of the company. In practice therefore the assessment of alternatives is at present fairly meaningless since developers will not identify an option likely to make profits for a competitor.

Scoping

Scoping is simply the part of the process when the applicant and the LPA decided what issues the EIA will investigate. The emphasis should be on the 'main' or 'significant' effects. Other issues may be of little or no significance for the particular development and will need only brief treatment to indicate that their relevance has been considered. Regulation 10 of the Regulations allows developers to obtain a formal scoping opinion from an LPA on what should be included in an ES. This is a controversial move because it throws a considerable administrative burden on planning officers. It also means that responsibility for failing to include an important issue rests as much with planning officers as it does with the applicant.

Baseline

The scoping exercise enables the applicant to establish the existing conditions or standards referred to as the baseline against which the effects of the proposed development may be judged. This can be crucial stage for communities who may have local knowledge which is highly relevant to understanding the base line conditions.

Consultation

As well as consulting the local authority anyone conducting an EIA is obliged to consult a set of statutory consultees. These names which included government agencies and laid down in regulation and are obliged to provide information which they held and which might be relevant to the EIA.

In practice there are some key consultees such as the Environment Agency who deal with a whole range of pollution issues and flood defence and English Nature and English Heritage who deal with biodiversity and archaeology respectively.

The consultation bodies are only required to provide information already in their possession usually held on public registers. They are not required to carry out any research on behalf of the applicant. A reasonable charge may be made to cover the cost of making the information available to the applicant.

In addition to the statutory consultation many of those working with third parties have taken the directive requirement for consultation as applying to the whole community placing a burden on the developers negotiating with local communities. In reality while this may be best practice UK EIA regulations do not require any additional level of public consultation. The applicant may however choose to consult other local organisations with a specific interest particularly where local groups or societies may have prepared species schedules and carry out regular monitoring.

Publicity

For an ES accompanying a planning application the publicity by the local planning authority consists of the following:

- A copy of the ES is put on Part I of the Register of Planning Applications available for inspection by members of the public
- A site notice in the prescribed form is displayed on or near the application site for not less than 21 days
- An advertisement is put in a newspaper circulating in the locality of the application site.

Where the development involved is likely to be controversial the planning authority may provide copies of the ES in local public libraries or at local authority offices or other convenient locations.

If an ES is submitted after the Planning Application it is the applicant's responsibility to organise publicity by:

- A notice that should be put in a newspaper circulating in the locality of the application site
- A site notice on the application site containing the same information as the newspaper advertisement, in a position where it is visible to members of the public without trespassing. The site notice should remain in position for not less than seven days in the month immediately preceding the submission of the ES.

A certificate that the site notice has been posted together with a copy of the newspaper advertisement should be supplied to the local planning authority with the ES.

1.15. What's the Format of an Environmental Statement?

Once the EIA has been carried out the information should be systematically presented in the environmental statement. The Regulations specify in Schedule 4 the information to be included in the ES is as follows:

Description of the development, including in particular:

- Description of the physical characteristics of the whole development and the land-use requirements during the construction and operational phases
- A description of the main characteristics of the production processes, for instance, nature and quantity of the materials used
- An estimate, by type and quantity, of expected residues and emissions (water, air and soil pollution, noise, vibration, light, heat, radiation, etc) resulting from the operation of the proposed development

A description of the aspects of the environment likely to be significantly affected by the proposed development, including in particular, population, fauna, flora, soil, water, air, climatic factors, material assets, including the architectural and archaeological heritage, landscape and the inter-relationship between the above factors. A description of the likely significant effects of the proposed development on the environment should cover the direct effects and any indirect, secondary, cumulative, short, medium and long-term, permanent and temporary, positive and negative effects of the development, resulting from:

- The existence of the development
- The use of the natural resources

- The emission of pollutants, the creation of nuisances and the elimination of waste and the description by the applicant of the forecasting methods used to assess the effects on the environment.

A description of the measures envisaged to prevent, reduce and where possible offset any significant adverse effects on the environment. A non-technical summary, of the information provided above. An indication of any difficulties (technical deficiencies or lack of know-how) encountered by the applicant in compiling the required information. There is no statutory or prescribed format for the arrangement of this information. This will depend upon the scale of the development project, and the complexity of the Issues that have been investigated. The ES can be a lengthy document with separate technical annexes.

At present, for an environmental statement of any significance it would be usual to provide the information on a CD-Rom.

An ES is often packaged in three parts:

Part I. The Planning Application

- Planning application form
- Certificate
- Schedule of plans and drawings

Part II. The Environmental Statement

1.16. Non-technical Summary

This is the summary of the contents and conclusions of the EIA. It is the part of the ES which may be published separately for circulation on a non-statutory, basis to local residents or interested parties. Beware of the often generalised nature of non technical summaries. If you really want to get grips with an application you need the full ES.

1.17. Environmental Statement

This sets out the information about the development in more detail than the non-technical summary. The ES draws together the threads which have been explored through the technical reports. These issues can be summarised tinder various headings, depending upon the nature of the development proposed, and having regard to the various items identified in the Regulations (see 6(1) Appointment of environmental consultants). It is necessary, to define the 'baseline' that has been adopted in order to demonstrate the effects, if any, of the development upon each key issue that has been identified by the scoping exercise. Also, where an issue has not been investigated in detail, this should be clearly explained in order to avoid any third party questioning the adequacy of the EIA. The mitigation measures should be described either in relation to each item or collated in a separate section of the ES which may also constitute the suggested environmental management and monitoring scheme to be followed during and after the development has been completed and is operational. The ES should set out an outline of the main alternatives studied by the applicant and an indication of the main reasons for his/her choice, taking into account the environmental effects.

Main alternatives may include:

- Physical location of sites
- Type of processes (where relevant)
- Physical appearance, design of buildings and site layout, including materials to be used
- Means of access including principal mode of transport to be used to gain access to the development

This component of an ES is often dealt with in a very summary way. It should not be ignored as it could give rise to third-party objections about the adequacy of the ES.

Part III: Technical Reports

The individual technical reports prepared for the various effects on the environment together with the data supporting the conclusions should be included in Part III. This enables the local planning authority to verify the contents of the ES by reference to the source material, and also be satisfied that the EIA has been sufficiently rigorous and in accordance with the methodology agreed as part of the scoping exercise.

1.18. When is an Environmental Statement not an Environmental Statement?

The format and contents of an ES can often be inadequate either in terms of the quality of the assessment or because key parts of the assessment are missing. Frequent defects include the failure to produce a non technical summary, the failure to adequately consider human health and the failure to include proper consideration of alternatives. The discussion above has outlined some of the issues which the regulations require EIA to consider. It's also worthwhile making reference to the original EU directive 97/11/EC which sometimes contains more useful indications of the scope of EIA.The legal principle of direct effect in which EU directives can have a direct effect in UK law, regardless of whether they have been transposed by UK regulations, means that local communities can mount challenges based on original directives.

1.19.   Are the Public Entitled to See the ES and how much should it Cost?

The public are entitled to see both the non technical summary and the full ES. The local planning authority is obliged to provide this information. The problem is that they are also entitled to make charges to copy material, which for a full ES might run into hundreds of pounds. The EIA regulations require that the developer must make available copies of the ES at a reasonable cost. This cost is nowhere defined but the average price for ES is between £60.00 and £120.00. This cost is a major barrier to public participation in the process. It is worth remembering that Parish Councils and elected members can often get free copies of ES. In the past some local groups have also obtained copies free through appealing to MPs or MEPs. Members of the public can rely on their rights under the Environmental Information Regulations 2004 to obtain copies of the document at no more than the cost of photocopying (see www.RightToKnowOnline.org). One way of saving costs is to ask for a copy of the EIA on a CD-Rom. Where the council has a copy in CD Rom format then this should cost no more than £1.00-£2.00 to obtain.

1.20.   What about Assessing the Quality of EIA

Information in planning cannot be seen as always providing a clear technical and objective statement of environmental circumstances. In practice the ES is often a sales document for the applicant and there have been increasing calls for an independent commission of EIAs to take them out of the hands of those with a vested interest in seeing schemes approved. This realisation is vitally important for the evaluation of EIA since it requires planners and the public to apply a critical assessment of both base line data and measures designed to secure mitigation. Beyond this critical mind set a number of formalised mechanisms have been developed with which to assess the quality of EIA. These methods are summarized in Appendix 7 of the DoE publication Good Practice on the Evaluation of environmental Information for Planning Projects (HMSO 1994). The most often used system is known as the Lee Colley review Package. This system attempts to divide an ES into its constituent areas and review categories and sub categories in line with an A to F scale. The review process is usually conducted by consultants with experience in each field but in fact any local community group could apply a technique particularly where they have local knowledge not possessed by the developer. The major problem with the system is that it's essentially subjective and certainly time consuming. It is therefore unlikely that a decision to reject the contents of ES could be justified solely on such an assessment. In practice the evaluation of ES is based on professional experience and on good knowledge of the application area and its environmental context.

The legal and procedural background to EIA is complex but members of the public can be surprisingly effective in participating in the process if they ignore the jargon, have a basic understanding of the process and apply their local knowledge effectively. Things to look out for are phrases such as "desk top survey" which is short hand for nobody had time to look at the site. The quality of ES can be surprisingly poor with developers often keen to do the least possible to get the application through so it is vital local people go on asking critical questions of the applicant and local authority planners. In the future EIA is likely to be applied to ever more forms of development. New measures will soon ensure the Strategic Environmental Assessment of planning policy and investment programmes. EIA can be made into a useful tool to defend the environmental quality of localities but only if local people feel able to engage with the process effectively.

CHAPTER II

THE EIA PROCESS OVERVIEW

2.1. Introduction

The EIA process makes sure that environmental issues are raised when a project or plan is first discussed and that all concerns are addressed as a project gains momentum through to implementation. Recommendations made by the EIA may necessitate the redesign of some project components, require further studies, suggest changes which alter the economic viability of the project or cause a delay in project implementation. To be of most benefit it is essential that an environmental assessment is carried out to determine significant impacts early in the project cycle so that recommendations can be built into the design and cost-benefit analysis without causing major delays or increased design costs. To be effective once implementation has commenced, the EIA should lead to a mechanism whereby adequate monitoring is undertaken to realize environmental management. An important output from the EIA process should be the delineation of enabling mechanisms for such effective management.

The way in which an EIA is carried out is not rigid: it is a process comprising a series of steps. These steps are outlined below and the techniques more commonly used in EIA are described in some detail in the section *Techniques*. The main steps in the EIA process are:

- Screening
- Scoping
- Impact analysis: prediction and mitigation
- Review and Decision-making
- Management and monitoring
- Audit

Figure shows a general flow diagram of the EIA process, how it fits in with parallel technical and economic studies and the role of public participation. In some cases, such as small-scale irrigation schemes, the transition from identification through to detailed design may be rapid and some steps in the EIA procedure may be omitted.

- **Screening** often results in a categorization of the project and from this a decision is made on whether or not a full EIA is to be carried out.

- **Scoping** is the process of determining which are the most critical issues to study and will involve community participation to some degree. It is at this early stage that EIA can most strongly influence the outline proposal.

- Detailed **prediction and mitigation** studies follow scoping and are carried out in parallel with the project feasibility studies.

- Public and statutory **review** of *Environmental Impact Statement* (EIS), and **decision** on whether to proceed or not, or to modify and resubmite the proposal.

- The main output report is called an *Environmental Impact Statement*, and contains a detailed plan for **managing and monitoring** environmental impacts both during and after implementation.

- Finally, an **audit** of the EIA process is carried out some time after implementation. The audit serves a useful feedback and learning function.

2.2.   Screening

Learning Outcomes of this Section

On successful completion of this Section, you will be able to:

- Understand the concept and explain why screening is necessary in EIA;
- Know how to undertake screening, including knowledge of procedures and project lists; and
- Be able to articulate the criteria determining the need for EIA.

Screening determines whether or not a proposal requires an EIA and, if so, what level of analysis is necessary. This process brings clarity and certainty to the implementation of the EIA, ensuring that it neither entails excessive review nor overlooks proposals that warrant examination. It is worth mentioning that a pre-screening consultation, though not normally taken as a part of a stage in the EA process, is recommended in recognition of its importance to enhance the overall effectiveness of the EA System. It is a stage where the proponent and the respective environmental or sectoral agencies establish contact and hold consultation on how best to proceed with the EA. It is advisable to do for it saves time and fosters a mutual understanding about the requirements.

2.3.   Purpose, Characteristics and Outcomes of Screening

Screening is the first key decision of the EIA process. Some type of screening procedure is necessary because of the large number of projects and activities that are potentially subject to EIA. The purpose of screening is to determine whether a proposal requires an EIA or not. It is intended to ensure that the form or level of any EIA review is commensurate with the importance of the issues raised by a proposal.

The conduct of screening thus involves making a preliminary determination of the expected impact of a proposal on the environment and of its relative significance. A certain level of basic information about the proposal and its location is required for this purpose. The time taken to complete the screening process will depend upon the type of proposal, the environmental setting and the degree of experience or understanding of its potential effects. Most proposals can be screened very quickly (in an hour or less) but some will take longer and a few will require an extended screening or initial assessment. Similarly, the majority of proposals may have little or no impacts and will be screened out of the EIA process. A smaller number of proposals will require further assessment. Only a limited number of proposals, usually major projects, will warrant a full EIA because they are known or considered to have potentially significant adverse impacts on the environment; for example, on human health and safety, on rare or endangered species, protected areas, fragile or valued ecosystems, biological diversity, air and water quality, or the lifestyle and livelihood of local communities.

The screening process can have one of four outcomes:

- No further level of EIA is required;
- A full and comprehensive EIA is required;
- A more limited EIA is required (often called a preliminary or initial assessment); or
- Further study is necessary to determine the level of EIA required (often called an initial environmental evaluation or examination [IEE]).

Screening establishes the basis for scoping, which identifies the key impacts to be studied and establishes the terms of reference for an EIA. Many EIA systems have formal screening and scoping procedures. In some cases, however, these terms may be used differently or applied at the discretion of the proponent. Also, on occasion, the screening and scoping stages may overlap, for example, when a further study (or IEE) is undertaken to determine whether or not the potential impacts are significant enough to warrant a full EIA.

2.4.   Screening Procedures and Methods

The requirements for screening and the procedure to be followed are often defined in the applicable EIA law or regulations (as in the Ethiopia EIA Procedural Guideline). In this guideline, the proposals to which EIA applies are listed in the annex. Usually, the proponent is responsible for carrying out screening, although this is done by the competent authority in some EIA systems. Whatever the requirements, screening should occur as early as possible in the development of the proposal so that the proponent and other participants are aware of the EIA obligations. It should be applied systematically and consistently (so that the same decisions would be reached if others conducted the screening process).

The screening procedures employed for this purpose can be classified into two broad, overlapping approaches:

- *Prescriptive or standardized approach-* proposals subject to or exempt from EIA are defined or listed in legislation and regulations; and
- *Discretionary or customized approach-* proposals are screened on an individual or case-by-case base, using indicative guidance.
  Specific methods used in screening include:
- Legal (or policy) definition of proposals to which EIA does or does not apply;
- Inclusion-list of projects (with or without thresholds) for which an EIA is automatically required;
- Exclusion-list of activities which do not require EIA because they are insignificant or are exempt by law (e.g. National security or emergency activities); and
- Criteria for case-by-case screening of proposals to identify those requiring an EIA because of their potentially significant environmental effects.

Both prescriptive and discretionary approaches have a place and their specific procedures can be combined into a comprehensive procedure (as shown in the diagram below). Where inclusive project lists are used, the disposition of most proposals will be immediately apparent. However, some proposals will be on the borderline in relation to a listed threshold and for others, the environmental impacts may be unclear or uncertain. In these situations, case-by-case screening should be undertaken, applying any indicative guidelines and criteria established for this purpose. This process gives the proponent or competent authority greater discretion than mandatory lists in determining the requirement for EIA.

2.5. Scoping

On successful completion of this Section, you will be able to:

- Understand and explain why scoping is necessary in EIA
- Know how to undertake scoping, including knowledge of different methods and approaches
- Consider and propose alternatives to a project
- Describe roles and requirements of baseline data in EIA studies
- Describe content of Terms of Reference, and outline boundaries for EIA studies.

Scoping stage is the process of interaction, which is a critical, early step in the preparation of an EIA. It identifies the issues that are likely to be of most importance during the EIA and eliminates those that are of little concern. Typically, this process concludes with the establishment of Terms of Reference for the preparation of an EIA. In this way, scoping ensures that EIA studies are focused on the significant effects and time and money are not wasted on unnecessary investigations.

The requirements and procedures of scoping established for this purpose differ from country to country. In many EIA systems, the involvement of the public, as well as the competent authority and other responsible government agencies, is an integral part of the scoping process. Public input helps to ensure that important issues are not overlooked when preparing Terms of Reference and/or initiating the EIA study. Scoping is aimed at identification of:

- Boundaries of the EIA studies
- Important issues of concerns
- Significant effects and factors to be considered

In addition, the scoping process can be used to help define the feasible alternatives to a proposed action. Not all EIA systems make provision for the generation or review of alternatives during scoping. These may follow, instead, from the issues that are identified as important. However, consideration of alternatives during scoping is becoming accepted internationally, as an EIA "good practice". The EIA Guideline of Ethiopia adopted this good practice.

Typically, scoping begins after the completion of the screening process. However, these stages may overlap to some degree. Essentially, scoping takes forward the preliminary determination of significance made in screening to the next stage of resolution, determining which issues and impacts are significant and require further study. In doing so, the scoping process places limits on the information to be gathered and analyzed in an EIA and focuses the approach to be taken.

The outcome of scoping is a scoping report or Terms of Reference (ToR)for undertaking full scale EA. Both of them require passing through reviewing process. The ToR This document sets out what the EIA is to cover, the type of information to be submitted and the depth of analysis that is required. It provides guidance to the proponent on how the study should be conducted and managed. Experience shows that the ToR should be a flexible document. The terms may need alteration as further information becomes available, and new issues emerge or others are reduced in importance.

2.6.   Roles and Objectives of Scoping

Scoping provides the foundations for an effective and efficient EIA process. When systematically carried out, scoping highlights the issues that matter and results in Terms of Reference for an EIA that provide clear direction to the proponent on what is required. This increases the likelihood of an adequately prepared EIA report. It helps to avoid the problem of unfocused, voluminous reports and the attendant delay while their deficiencies are addressed and corrected. Scoping thereby helps to make sure that resources are targeted on collecting the information necessary for decision-making and not wasted on undertaking the excessive analysis.

The scoping process itself can vary in scope, complexity and time taken. A comprehensive approach to scoping may be needed for large-scale proposals, which have a range of impacts that are potentially significant. In other cases, scoping will be a more limited and restricted exercise. Depending on the circumstances, the scoping process can be tailored to include some or all of the aims listed below. Key objectives of scoping are to:

- Inform the public about the proposal;
- Identify the main stakeholders and their concerns and values;
- Define the reasonable and practical alternatives to the proposal;
- Focus the important issues and significant impacts to be addressed by an EIA;
- Define the boundaries for an EIA in time, space and subject matter;
- Set requirements for the collection of baseline and other information; and
- Establish the Terms of Reference for an EIA study.
- Guiding Principle and Elements of Scoping

Guiding principles for carrying out the scoping process include the following:

- Recognize scoping is a process rather than a discrete activity or event;
- Design the scoping process for each proposal, taking into account the environment and people affected;
- Start scoping as soon as you have sufficient information available;
- Prepare an information package or circular explaining the proposal and the process;
- Specify the role and contribution of the stakeholders and the public;
- Take a systematic approach but implement flexibly;
- Document the results to guide preparation of an EIA; and
- Respond to new information and further issues raised by stakeholders.

The elements of scoping differs to some degree with the EIA requirements established by different countries and international agencies (See the EIA guidelines of Ethiopia). A comprehensive scoping process will include all or a combination of the following functions:

- Identify the range of community and scientific concerns about a proposed project or action;
- Evaluate these concerns to identify the significant issues (and to eliminate those issues which are not important); and
- Organize and prioritize these issues to focus the information that is critical for decision making, and that will be studied in detail in the next phase of EIA.

A systematic and transparent approach should be taken to sifting and paring down the concerns, issues and impacts. This can be undertaken in three steps:

- Compile a "long list" of concerns from the information available and the inputs of stakeholders. No attempt should be made at this stage to exclude or pre-judge concerns.
- Derive a "short list" of key issues and problem areas based on their potential significance and likely importance for decision-making on the proposal. This phase involves evaluating the issues against selected criteria; for example, differentiating serious risks or threats from effects that can be mitigated.
- Classify and order the key issues into "impact categories" by reference to policy objectives and scientific concepts, such as emission levels that may exceed health or environmental standards. Such a synthesis or aggregation provides a coherent framework for drafting the Terms of Reference for the EIA study.

The table below contains an indicative list of activities to be carried out when scoping in accordance with this approach. The list begins with "getting ready" by preparing a profile of the scope under key headings and using this as a basis for informal consultations with key stakeholders. Once this round of discussion has occurred, the three steps described above take place with iterations between them. Finally, the Terms of Reference are established, with provision for adjustment and feedback as and when necessary during the EIA process.

In practice, the first phase of scoping, opening out the list of concerns and issues, is much easier to achieve than the next two. With few exceptions, most EIA systems experience difficulties in narrowing down and focusing on the issues that matter. This imposes certain limitations when preparing Terms of Reference, with potential knock on effects on the next stage of work on the EIA study. Ultimately, it is the responsibility of the proponent or competent authority to bring the scoping process to a conclusion.

Activity	Items
Getting ready	1. Prepare a preliminary or outline scope with headings such as: • objectives and description of the proposal • the policy context and environmental setting • data and information sources, constraints etc. • alternatives to the proposal • concerns, issues and effects identified to date • provision for public involvement • timetable for scoping, EIA and decision making
	2. Develop the outline scope by informal consultation and by assembling available information, identifying information gaps, etc.
	3. Make the provisional scope and supporting information available to the public.
Undertaking scoping	4. Draw up a long list of the range of issues and concerns.
	5. Evaluate their relative importance and significance to derive a short list of key issues.
	6. Organize the key issues into the impact categories to be studied.
Completion and continuity	7. Amend the outline scope to progressively incorporate the information from each stage.
	8. Establish the Terms of Reference for the EIA, including information requirements, study guidelines, methodology and protocols for revising work.
	9. Monitor progress against the ToR, making adjustments as needed and provide feedback to stakeholders and the public.

2.7. Methods Used in Scoping

Depending upon the EIA system, responsibility for scoping may lie with the proponent, with the competent authority, or with the EIA agency or an independent body set up for the purpose. In many cases, some form of guidance will be given on the conduct of scoping, the procedures to be followed and the methods that can be used to undertake the consultative and technical components of this activity. For specific proposals, it may be possible to draw upon previous experience, represented by existing scoping documentation for a similar proposal, or generic or sector guidelines and checklists. None of these aids, however, replace the need for designing a scoping process for each proposal and its likely consequences.

A custom-tailored scoping process will include an overview or profile of the proposal, the environment and community that is likely to be affected, the possible alternatives, the range of potential impacts, and the ways these may be mitigated or managed. In addition, the following should be addressed:

- Geographical area(s) and the time-frame(s) for impact analysis;
- The policy and institutional frameworks under which the EIA will be conducted;
- Existing information sources, gaps and constraints on methodology;

- The scheduling of the EIA study, and the allocation of resources and responsibilities; and

- The relationship to the decision-making process, including modification of design and selection of alternatives," as well as final approval of the proposal.

The use of impact models or cause-effect frameworks may be helpful during scoping of large-scale proposals, which have a wide range of potentially complex effects on the environment. But they can also have value in other cases where it is sometimes easy to overlook long-term and secondary impacts of proposals. For example, waste discharged into the air or waterways can extend a long way beyond the boundaries of a project, and heavy metals can bio-accumulate in species and food chains. The identification of such potential impacts can be assisted by a systematic consideration of the various phases of the project life cycle, from construction through operation to decommissioning. The proposed plan for public involvement in the EIA process (including scoping) should be ready (see Module 3) used in for informing and involving the public.

Although scoping is a distinct, early process within EIA, the significant effects continue to be re-interpreted throughout an EIA study, the decision-making process and project implementation and monitoring.

Stakeholders in Scoping

Stakeholders	Possible Roles
Proponent/competent authority	Know most about the proposal, and have a strongly developed view about the factors that will influence the site selection and other aspects of decision making. The scoping process helps proponents to recognize the perspective of others, to consider alternatives and concerns of those affected, and to make changes to the proposal, which will address these inputs.
EIA administering body	Generally establish and oversee statutory or procedural requirements for scoping, including the matters to be addressed, the people to be consulted, and the form of consultation. It approves the EIA report submitted by the proponent, checking it against the agreed scope.
Other responsible agencies	Contribute relevant information about specific issues and matters within their jurisdiction. This information may include specific legislative requirements, policy objectives, and standards, technical knowledge and expertise, and experience with similar projects or local conditions. They may provide licenses, permits, approvals or leases..
EIA practitioners and experts	May act directly for the agencies involved or for the proponent as consultants retained for the EIA work, or they may function in an advisory or review capacity on behalf of scientific, NGO or professional bodies. Their involvement can be of particular value in providing specialist knowledge.
People affected by the proposal	Have a major role in identifying concerns and issues and providing local knowledge and information. Their views should be taken into account in choosing between alternatives, in deciding on the importance of issues, and in identifying mitigating measures, compensation provisions and management plans.
Wider community	will also provide information and views that are relevant to scoping. This grouping includes those indirectly affected by the proposal, and local, national and sometimes international NGOs and interest groups..

By involving the public, scoping helps to build confidence in the EIA process. Often, the scoping process is the first major point of contact with the stakeholders who are affected by or interested in the proposal and the alternatives.

Alternatives

The consideration of alternatives to a proposal is a requirement of many EIA systems. It lies at the heart of the EIA process and methodology. During the scoping process, alternatives to a proposal can be generated or refined, either directly or by reference to the key issues identified. A comparison of alternatives will help to determine the best method of achieving project objectives while minimizing environmental impacts or, more creatively, indicate the most environmentally friendly or best practicable environmental option.

Often, however, the consideration of alternatives is a superficial rather than a meaningful exercise. This is particularly true of private sector proposals, where the requirement to analyze alternatives is less than for comparable public sector proposals. It is also true of all proposals that are submitted to EIA when planning is nearly complete and the components and location are fixed already. This practice is becoming less and less acceptable as EIA matures and as sustainability issues and cumulative effects take on greater importance.

The consideration of alternatives is likely to be most useful when the EIA is undertaken early in the project cycle. Depending on timing, the type and range of alternatives open for consideration might include (also see table below):

- Demand alternatives (e.g. using energy more efficiently rather than building more generating capacity);
- Input or supply alternatives (e.g. where a mix of energy sources permits);
- Activity alternatives (e.g. providing public transport rather than increasing road capacity);
- Location alternatives, either for the entire proposal or for components (e.g. the location of a dam and/or irrigation channels);
- Process alternatives (e.g. use of waste-minimizing or energy-efficient technology); and
- Scheduling alternatives (e.g. for airport and transport operations, reservoir drawdown).

The development of feasible alternatives, to meet the overall objectives of the proposal calls for certain types of information and knowledge. During this process, for example, reference may be made to: available technology, policy objectives, social attitudes, environmental and site constraints and project economics, as demonstrated in the case study of the Hydropower Project in the annex. It is important to make sure that the alternatives chosen for comparison with a proposal can be implemented cost-effectively. Stakeholder input can be helpful in the generation and analysis of viable alternatives, but this needs to be used selectively.

The range of alternatives selected for analysis routinely includes the 'no action' alternative. The relative impact of each alternative is compared against the baseline environment (with versus without the project) to select a preferred alternative, including taking no action (which may not correspond exactly to maintaining baseline conditions because changes result from other actions).

Examples of Alternatives

Proposed Project	Alternative	Category
A. Coal fired power station near a major city.	1. Hydropower station in highlands.	Input/location
	2. Located away from the city near the river	Location
	3. Energy efficiency programme.	Demand
B. Upgrading of a road to a dual carriage way.	1. Investment in public transport.	Activity
	2. Construction of relief road	Location
	3. Phased construction of road.	Scheduling
C. 5000 ha irrigation scheme to increase food production	1. Rehabilitation of existing small-scale irrigation schemes	Activity/location
	Improved rain-fed agricultural systems.	Process/location

2.8. EIA Terms of Reference

In concluding the scoping process, the preparation of Terms of Reference (ToR) for an EIA is an important task. Alternatively, or as a supplement to ToR, a formal scoping report may be issued (described below as agartad from EPA, Ethiopia). In some EIA systems, the proponent prepares a more informal document to summarize the conclusions of scoping and the approach to be taken by an EIA study. The test for Terms of Reference (or its equivalent) lies in its usefulness to and robustness in successive stages of the EIA process.

A number of international agencies have issued sample or framework Terms of Reference, including the OECD Development Assistance Committee and the World Bank. These and other generic documents outline the types of information to be included in a ToR or equivalent document. When reviewing these, it is important to remember that Terms of Reference provide guidance and direction to the proponent. The document should be comprehensive yet as concise as possible. Scoping report should include as a minimum:

- a brief description of the project,
- all alternatives identified,
- issues raised by IAPs

- description of the public participation,

EPA of Ethiopia issued the outline of a ToR for EIA, as listed below.

- Background to the proposal,
- Setting the context of the problem,
- Consideration of alternatives,
- Institutional and public involvement,
- Required information regarding project and location, etc,,
- Analysis of impacts,
- Mitigation and monitoring, and
- Conclusions and recommendations,

2.9. Baseline Studies

Baseline studies using available data and local knowledge will be required for scoping. Once key issues have been identified, the need for further in-depth studies can be clearly identified and any additional data collection initiated. The International Commission on Irrigation and Drainage (ICID) *Check-list* will be found useful to define both coarse information required for scoping and further baseline studies required for prediction and monitoring. Specialists, preferably with local knowledge, will be needed in each key area identified. They will need to define further data collection, to ensure that it is efficient and targeted to answer specific questions, and to quantify impacts. A full year of baseline data is desirable to capture seasonal effects of many environmental phenomena. However, to avoid delay in decision making, short-term data monitoring should be undertaken in parallel with long-term collection to provide conservative estimates of environmental impacts.

Definitions

Baseline information data is the starting point or level of a particular social, biophysical and economic variable against which subsequent changes can be detected and/or predicted through monitoring".

Baseline survey refers to the collection of background information on the environmental and socio-economic setting for a proposed development project.

Baseline monitoring is the measurement of environmental parameters during a representative pre-project period in an attempt to determine the nature and ranges of natural variation and where possible to establish the process of change. NB This will often continue into project operation as part of environmental monitoring. Impact predictions are made against a "baseline" established by the existing environment (or by its future state). In many cases, however, it is likely that the current baseline conditions will still exist when a project is implemented. In these cases, predictions may need to be made about the future state of the environment (the baseline condition for the no-development option), which is baseline monitoring.

Baseline Monitoring is Important

- When potential interactions between project and environment are not well understood;
- When project implementation methods have not been clearly defined, or are experimental, or are subject to change;
- When the potential impacts on the natural or social environment are controversial;
- When project scheduling is subject to change so that impacts could be more serious than originally predicted.

Baseline Data Collection

Variable of the baseline data can be constant, variable, declining or increasing.

Methods: formal (scientific, surveys, measurement) and informal (local knowledge, traditional etc.).

Type: primary (new, direct), secondary (old, reference data, reports) and remote (e.g. air photos, satellite images) or on the ground

Issues: Costs of surveys, Time required and Reliability of information

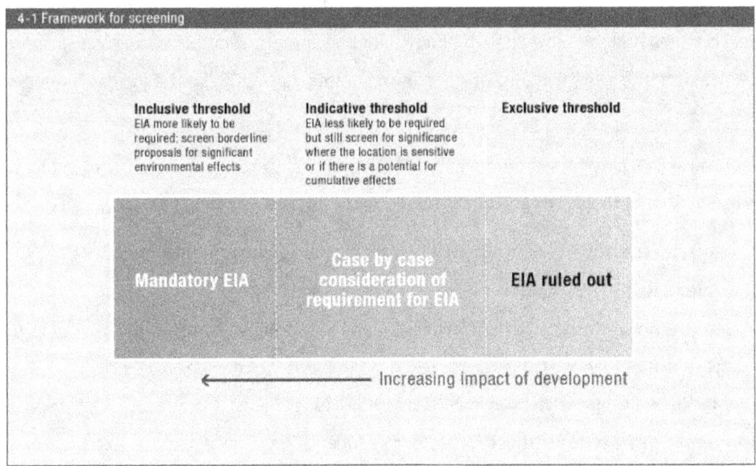

In this context, screening is a flexible process and can be extended into preliminary forms of EIA study. These "extended screening" procedures include:

- **Initial environmental examination**- carried out in cases where the environmental impacts of a proposal are uncertain or unknown (e.g. new technologies or undeveloped areas);

- **Environmental overview**- carried out as a rapid assessment of the environmental issues and impacts of a proposal; and

- **Class screening**- carried out for a family of small projects or repetitive activities, where the environmental effects and means of mitigation are known but there is potential for cumulative impacts (e.g. dredging, road realignment, bank stabilization).

2.10. Project Lists for Screening

Project lists are widely used to screen proposals. These lists are of two types. Most are "inclusion" lists, which describe the project types and size thresholds that are known or considered to have significant or serious environmental impacts. Usually, listed projects that fall within these predetermined thresholds will be subject automatically to full and comprehensive EIA. Some EIA systems also maintain "exclusion" lists of activities that are exempt because they are known to have little or no environmental impact. The inclusion lists used by countries and international organizations differ in content, comprehensiveness, threshold levels and requirements for mandatory application. In certain EIA systems, scale thresholds are specified for each type of listed project for which an EIA is mandatory. Other projects that may require an EIA are screened individually against environmental significance criteria, such as emission levels or proximity to sensitive and protected areas. Internationally and nationally, reference is often made to:

Use of these lists is reported by the EPA of Ethiopia to be a reliable aid to the classification of proposals into one of three categories (See table below and the Guideline for the detail):

- Projects requiring a full EIA because of their likely environmental effects;
- Projects Requiring Initial Invironmental examination; and
- Projects not requiring further environmental analysis (for example health and nutrition, institutional and human resource development and technical assistance).

Listed projects provide a standardized framework for screening proposals. This approach is simple to apply, at least in its most basic form of identifying the type and size of project for which EIA is mandatory or almost certainly required. However, project lists should be used cautiously and with due regard to their weaknesses, especially if they are the sole basis for screening.

World Bank and international experience indicates that project lists should be used flexibly in screening proposals. Reference should be made to the location and setting of the proposal, as well as its scale. A low-head hydropower dam or small-scale quarry (<100 ha) normally would not merit full EIA. However, the proposal may need to be reclassified if it is located in or near sensitive and valued ecosystems, or heritage resources, displaces people who are particularly vulnerable and difficult to resettle or has evident cumulative impacts (e.g. one of a series of quarries or dams). The methods available for this purpose are discussed below.

Category	Projects	Projects
Projects Requiring Full EIA	<ul><li>Water management projects for agriculture (drainage, irrigation)</li><li>Large scale mono- culture (cash and food crops)</li><li>Fertilizer and nutrient managemen</li><li>Construction of wastewater treatment plant</li><li>Construction of marine out fall</li><li>Night soil collection transport and treatment</li><li>Ccanalization of water courses</li><li>Diversion of normal flow of water</li><li>Water transfers scheme</li><li>Abstraction or utilization of ground and surface water for bulk supply</li><li>Water treatment plants</li><li>Construction of dams, impounding reservoirs with a surface area of 100 hec</li></ul>	<ul><li>Timber logging and processing</li><li>Medium to large scale fisheries</li><li>Artificial fisheries</li><li>Hydro-electric power</li><li>Biomass power development</li><li>Wind -mills power development</li><li>River drainage and flood control works.</li><li>Hydro - electric and irrigation dams</li><li>Reservoir</li><li>Construction of waste water treatment plant (off-site)</li><li>Construction of secure land fills facility</li><li>Ground water development for industrial, agricultural or urban water supply of greater than 4000 m3 /day</li><li>Drainage Plans in towns close to water bodies</li></ul>
Projects Requiring a Preliminary Environmetal Examinations	<ul><li>Fish culture</li><li>Bee-keeping</li><li>Small animal husbandry and urban livestock keeping</li><li>Horticulture and floriculture</li><li>Wildlife catching and trading</li><li>Production of tourist handicrafts</li><li>Brewing and distilleries</li><li>Bio-gas plants</li></ul>	<ul><li>Charcoal production</li><li>Fuel wood harvesting</li><li>Wooden furniture and implement making</li><li>Basket and other weaving</li><li>Nuts and seeds for oil processing</li><li>Bark for tanning processing</li><li>Rain water harvesting</li></ul>
Projects may not Require EIA	<ul><li>Educational facilities (small scale)</li><li>Audio visual production</li><li>Teaching facilities and equipment</li><li>Training</li><li>Medical centre (small scale)</li><li>Medical supplies and equipment</li><li>Nutrition</li><li>Family planning</li></ul>	<ul><li>Surface water fed irrigation projects covering less than 50 hectares</li><li>Ground water fed irrigation projects covering less than 50 hectares</li><li>All small scale agricultural activities</li></ul>

Case-by-Case Screening

Case-by-case screening is carried out when the significance of the potential environmental impact of a proposal is unclear or uncertain. This process typically applies to proposals that fall just below or close to the thresholds established for the listed projects. In addition, non-borderline proposals may be subject to screening if they are located in sensitive areas or there is a potential for cumulative effects in combination with other current and foreseeable activities. The framework outlined above in this course contains a sieve of screening applications with a progressively finer mesh for including proposals. It has gained a degree of international acceptance as a standard of good practice. The specific criteria for case-by-case screening differ from country to country. Typically, however, they are based on a number of common factors related to the consideration of the significance of environmental impacts. These include the location of proposals, environmental sensitivity and any likely health and social effects on the local population. In this context, reference may be made to the screening criteria listed in the Ethiopian EIA guideline (Annex II), a criteria which may be adapted to wider use in case-by-case screening. A proposal can be tested for significance by taking account of:

- Located near to protected or designated areas or within landscapes of special heritage value;
- Existing land use(s) and commitments;
- The relative abundance, quality and *regenerative capacity* of natural resources;
- The *absorption capacity* of the natural environment, paying particular attention to wetlands, coastal zones, mountain and forest areas; and
- Areas in which the *environmental quality standards laid down in law have been exceeded already*.

2.11. Extended Screening or Preliminary EIA

Certain proposals may be subject to an extended-screening or initial assessment (also called a preliminary EIA). Such an approach can be used when the requirement for EIA could not be reasonably determined by the application of the screening procedures described previously; for example when a proposal involves use of a new technology or is located in a near natural or frontier area or involves discharges into a water body that may exceed health or environmental standards. Often, this process, itself, may be sufficient to complete the requirement for EIA established by a particular country. In this case, a screening report should describe the results and identify any mitigation measures or actions that need to be taken.

When undertaking this type of preliminary EIA study, the proponent or competent authority may need to assemble considerable information. A checklist of the types of information that could be relevant for such a a preliminary EIA study includes:

- A description of the proposal;
- Applicable policies, plans and regulations, including environmental standards and objectives;
- The characteristics of the environment, including land use, significant resources, critical ecological functions, pollution and emission levels etc.;
- The potential impacts of the proposal and their likely significance;
- The degree of public concern and interest about the proposal.

This is accompanied by a framework of criteria and questions that can help in the conduct of a preliminary EIA. The following paragraphs describe screening criteria based on Annex II of the guideline,). The potential adverse impacts of concern during the screening process are as follows:

- **Socio-economic impacts:** falling living standards, particularly of the poor, could risk the start of a vicious circle that could produce further environmental degradation. Living and working conditions may deteriorate as a result of such processes as resettlement, cultural shock, risk to health and safety, the intrusion on sight, sound and smell, etc. Impacts on men and women may be very different, impacts will also vary between social groups, especially where rights to land and other natural resources are differentiated. In-migration related to project development could cause important social changes.
- **Degradation of land and aquatic environments:** major changes in land-use, deforestation, watershed degradation, loss of biodiversity, soil erosion, dry land degradation and overgrazing, salinization, water logging and land-based pollution are all impacts of concern.
- **Water Pollution:** pollution of water courses, aquifers, water bodies and coasts can result from uncontrolled wastewater/sewage discharge from human settlements, industrial effluent, agricultural chemicals, etc.
- **Air pollution:** pollution of the air may be caused by urban traffic, pollutants may be odour, smell, dust, sulphurdioxide, oxides of nitrogen, ammonia or even storage of volatile liquids, routine industrial emission, upset industrial conditions, etc.

- **Noise and/or vibration:** noise and vibration will be caused by any rotating or reciprocating machinery, but will also be associated with blasting, excavating equipment, road traffic, entertainment, etc

- **Damage to wildlife and habitat:** impacts that affect biodiversity, ecosystems, rare or endangered species or flora/fauna having economic or scientific importance.

- **Alterations to ecological processes:** e.g. energy transfer bio-accumulation, etc.

- **Effects on cultural, religious, historic, archaeological and scientific resources**: including the effects of in-migrants or tourists

- **Climate, especially the hydrological cycle.**

- **Impacts on human health.**

2.12. Initial Environmental Evaluation or Examination (IEE)

In some EIA systems, an IEE is required when the potential environmental impacts of a proposal cannot be established by the application of standard screening procedures. Typically, an IEE is a relatively low-cost analysis that makes use of information already available. It is carried out using EIA procedures and methods, which are scaled to purpose. For example, key issues can be identified by a rapid scoping exercise, based on consultation with local people and agencies. A site or area visit should take place to survey the current situation and obtain "baseline" information. Simple methods, such as a checklist or matrix, are used in impact identification and often focus on appropriate mitigation measures. Depending on its findings, the IEE report can be used either as a scoping document when a proposal is referred to a full EIA or to support environmentally sound planning and design when a proposal does not require further review. An IEE is a preliminary EIA study that:

- Describes the proposal and the environmental setting;
- Considers alternatives to improve the environmental benefits;
- Addresses the concerns of the local community;
- Identifies the potential environmental effects;
- Identifies measures to mitigate adverse impacts; and
- Describes, as necessary, environmental monitoring and management plans.

2.13. Mitigation and Impact Management

Mitigation is a critical component of the EIA process. It aims to prevent adverse impacts from happening and to keep those that do occur within an acceptable level. Opportunities for impact mitigation will occur throughout the project cycle.

The objectives of mitigation are to:

Mitigation seeks to:

- Find better ways of doing things,
- Minimize or eliminate negative impacts,
- Enhance benefits, and
- Protect public and individual rights to compensation,

Early links should be established between the EIA and project design teams to identify mitigation opportunities and incorporate them into consideration of alternatives and design options. In practice, mitigation is emphasised in the EIA process once the extent of the potential impact of a proposal is reasonably well understood. This typically takes place following impact identification and prediction, and recommended measures for mitigation will be an important part of the EIA report. Usually, these measures will be incorporated into the terms and conditions of project approval and implemented during the impact management stage of the EIA process.

The objectives of impact management are to:

- Ensure that mitigation measures are implemented;
- Establish systems and procedures for this purpose;
- Monitor the effectiveness of mitigation measures; and
- Take any necessary action when unforeseen impacts occur.

The adverse impacts and consequences of a proposal can occur far beyond the site boundaries of a project. In the past, many of the real costs of development proposals were not accounted for in economic analyses of project feasibility, particularly in the operational and decommissioning phases of the project cycle. As a result, these costs were borne by the community affected or the public at large rather than by the proponent.

Stricter requirements are now being imposed on proponents to:

- Mitigate impacts through good project design and environmental management;
- Provide benefits to the community affected by the proposal;
- Prepare plans for managing impacts so these are kept within acceptable levels; and
- Make good any residual environmental damage.

The responsibility of proponents to "internalize" the full environmental costs of development proposals is now widely accepted. In addition, many proponents have found that good design and impact management can result in significant savings. This outcome is similar to that found in industries applying the principles of cleaner production to improve their environmental performance.

The sustainability agenda is placing new demands on proponents with regard to mitigation and impact management. For example, increasing attention is being given to the principle of "no net loss of natural and social capital". Under the polluter pays principle, the application of this principle could require the proponent to make restitution for unavoidable residual damages. In this case, mitigation would include in-kind compensation measures, comprising equivalent, comparable or suitable offsets for all residual environmental impacts of a proposal.

2.14. EIA Stage for Considering Mitigation

In the EIA Report the section for mitigation measures is often located after the evaluation section, that is after the analysis and comparison of alternatives has been reported. This gives the impression that first a preferred alternative has been selected, then second mitigating measures have been added to the project. This process may seem to be appropriate, but unless there has been a subsequent review of the alternatives the chosen one, with mitigation measures, may be a worse option. In particular the mitigation measures will add costs to the preferred alternative. It could be that in total the cost becomes greater than a second alternative that had less impact on the environment. In this situation the second alternative would have been preferable to the one chosen having both less impact and being less cost.

Consequently, the stage for thinking about mitigation measures should be before there has been a comparison of the alternatives. The point of considering safeguards before comparision is to encourage the analyst to think about the "extras" that may have to be added onto the basic proposal, before the evaluation of the proposal is undertaken. This will help to ensure that the comparison, or evaluation, of alternatives is conducted when all the relevant information and costs are included. A crucial point to remember is that after safeguards are added to a proposal, the alternatives may become more attractive (eg cheaper).

Main Elements of Mitigation

In Figure below, the elements of mitigation are organised into a hierarchy of actions:

- First, avoid adverse impacts as far as possible by use of preventative measures;
- Second, minimise or reduce adverse impacts to "as low as practicable" levels; and
- Third, remedy or compensate for adverse residual impacts, which are unavoidable and cannot be reduced further.

A three-step process of mitigation can be applied to relate the hierarchy of elements in Figure (below) to the stages of the EIA process when they are typically applied. Generally, as project design becomes more detailed, the opportunities for impact avoidance narrow and the concern is to minimise and compensate for unavoidable impacts. However, these distinctions are not rigid and opportunities for creative mitigation should be sought at all stages of EIA and project planning.

The Elements of Mitigation

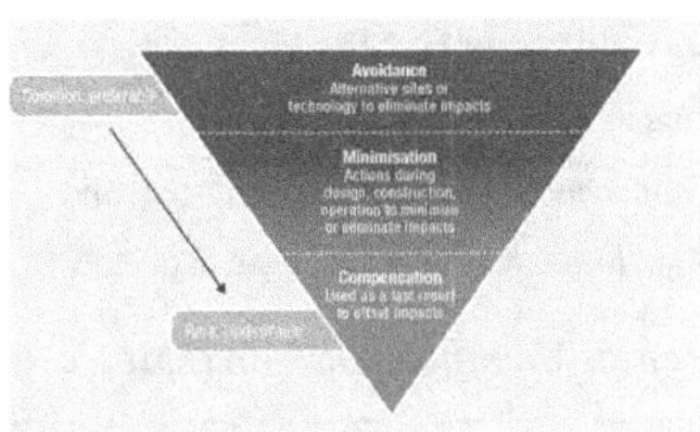

Impact Monitoring and Management

Mitigation measures are implemented as part of impact management. This process is accompanied by monitoring to check that impacts are "as predicted". When unforeseen impacts or problems occur, they can require corrective action to keep them within acceptable levels, thereby changing the mitigation measures recommended in an EIA or set out in an environmental management report.

In some cases, it may be necessary to establish or strengthen impact management systems to facilitate the implementation of mitigation measures during project construction and operation. These supporting actions should be identified as part of the environmental management plan. They can include the establishment of an environmental management system (EMS) based upon ISO 14000 guidelines for strengthening particular arrangements for impact management. Any other supporting actions to implement these measures, such as training and capacity building, should also be specified.

2.15. Environmental Management Plan and Mitigation Measures

An environmental management plan (EMP), also referred to as an impact management plan, is usually prepared as part of EIA reporting. It translates recommended mitigation and monitoring measures into specific actions that will be carried out by the proponent. Depending upon particular requirements, the plan may be included in, or appended to, the EIA report or may be a separate document. The EMP will need to be adjusted to the terms and conditions specified in any project approval. It will then form the basis for impact management during project construction and operation.

The main components of an EMP are described in the table below, which reflects practice at the World Bank. Although there is no standard format, the EMP should contain:

- summary of the potential impacts of the proposal;
- description of the recommended mitigation measures;
- statement of their compliance with relevant standards;
- allocation of resources and responsibilities for plan implementation;
- schedule of the actions to be taken;
- programme for surveillance, monitoring and auditing; and
- contingency plan when impacts are greater than expected.

Contents of an Environmental Management Plan (EMP)

EMP Component	How to address
Source: World Bank, 1999	
Summary of impacts	The predicted adverse environmental and social impacts for which mitigation is required should be identified and briefly summarised. Cross referencing to the EA report or other documentation is recommended.
Description of mitigation measures	Each mitigation measure should be briefly described with reference to the impact to which it relates and the conditions under which it is required (for example, continuously or in the event of contingencies). These should be accompanied by, or referenced to, project design and operating procedures which elaborate on the technical aspects of implementing the various measures.
Description of monitoring programme	The monitoring program should clearly indicate the linkages between impacts identified in the EIA report, measurement indicators, detection limits (where appropriate), and definition of thresholds that will signal the need for corrective actions.
Institutional arrangements	Responsibilities for mitigation and monitoring should be clearly defined, including arrangements for co-ordination between the various actors responsible for mitigation.
Implementation schedule and reporting procedures	The timing, frequency and duration of mitigation measure should be specified in an implementation schedule, showing links with overall project implementation. Procedures to provide information on the progress and results of mitigation and monitoring measures should also be clearly specified.
Cost estimates and sources of funds	These should be specified for both the initial investment and recurring expenses for implementing all measures contained in the EMP, integrated into the total project costs, and factored into loan negotiations.

The EMP should contain commitments that are binding on the proponent. It can be translated into project documentation and provide the basis for a legal contract that sets out the responsibilities of the proponent. In turn, the proponent can use the EMP to establish environmental performance standards and requirements for those carrying out the works or providing supplies. An EMP can also be used to prepare an environmental management system for the operational phase of the project.

The main components of an EMP, according to the EPA's EIA Procedural Guideline of Ethiopia, should include:

- state policy and standards,
- indicate environmental effects, the issue and activity required to address it,
- define responsibilities, provide a schedule of tasks,
- include a system of reporting,
- include a system for monitoring and auditing,
- indicate resources required for completion and where relevant actual costs, including training and equipment needs,
- describe the proposed mitigation measures,
- contain a contingency plan, etc.

2.16. EIA Reporting and Review

A number of different names are used for the report that is prepared on the findings of the EIA process. The generic term "EIA report" is used here. Other terms commonly used for the same document include environmental impact statement (EIS) and environmental statement (ES). Further variations may be introduced by the terminology used in different countries. Despite the different names, EIA reports have the same basic purpose, approach and structure. Usually, the proponent is responsible for the preparation of the EIA report. The information contained in the report should meet the terms of reference established at the scoping stage of the EIA process. The purpose of the EIA report is to provide a coherent statement of the potential impacts of a proposal and the measures that can be taken to reduce and remedy them. It contains essential information for:

- the proponent to implement the proposal in an environmentally and socially responsible way;
- the responsible authority to make an informed decision on the proposal, including the terms and conditions that must be attached to an approval or authorisation; and

- the public to understand the proposal and its likely impacts on people and the environment.

A successful EIA report that meets these aims will be:

- actionable-a document that can be applied by the proponent to achieve environmentally sound planning and design;
- decision-relevant-a document that organises and presents the information necessary for project authorisation and, if applicable, permitting and licensing; and
- user- friendly-a document that communicates the technical issues to all parties in a clear and comprehensible way.

Typical Elements of an EIA Report

In many countries, the information to be included in an EIA report is specified in legislation, procedure or guidance. In addition to what is specified in the ToR, the EIA report may include additional issues and other matters that have emerged as a result of EIA studies and need to be taken into account in decision-making.

An EIA report typically includes many or all of the following headings and items:

- executive or non-technical summary (which may be used as a public communication document);
- statement of the need for, and objectives of, the proposal;
- reference to applicable legislative, regulatory and policy frameworks;
- description of the proposal and how it will be implemented (construction, operation and decommissioning);
- comparison of the proposal and the alternatives to it (including the no action alternative);
- description of the project setting, including the relationship to other proposals, current land-uses and relevant policies and plans for the area;
- description of baseline conditions and trends (biophysical, socioeconomic etc), identifying any changes anticipated prior to project implementation;
- review of the public consultation process, the views and concerns expressed by stakeholders and the way these have been taken into account;
- consideration of the main impacts (positive and adverse) that are identified as likely to result from the proposal, their predicted characteristics (e.g. magnitude, occurrence,

timing, etc.) proposed mitigation measures, the residual effects and any uncertainties and limitations of data and analysis;

- evaluation of the significance of the residual impacts, preferably for each alternative, with an identification of the best practicable environmental option;
- an environmental management plan that identifies how proposed mitigation and monitoring measures will be translated into specific actions as part of impact management[1]; and
- appendices containing supporting technical information, description of methods used to collect and analyse data, list of references, etc.

2.17. Executive or Non-technical Summary

The executive summary gives a concise description of the main findings and recommendations. It is not meant to summarise all of the contents of the EIA report. Instead the focus is on the key information and options for decision-making. Except for very large proposals, the executive summary should be kept short, no more than seven pages and preferably less. Often, the executive summary is the only part of the report that decision makers and most people will read. It can be written for distribution to the public as an information brochure.

An executive summary should describe:

- The proposal and its setting;
- The terms of reference for the EIA;
- The results of public consultation;
- The alternatives considered;
- Major impacts and their significance;
- Proposed mitigation measures;
- The environmental management plan; and
- Any other critical matters that bear on the decision.

Need and objectives of the proposal: A clear statement of the need for and objectives of the proposal should be given. Typically, need is substantiated by reference to relevant policies and plans. Reference also can be made to the demands and issues that the proposal is intended to address, the purpose that will be achieved, and the benefits that are anticipated.

Legal and policy framework: There is usually a brief description of the legal and policy framework that applies to the proposal being assessed. Relevant aspects of EIA procedure can be cited, together with any other requirements or considerations that need to be mentioned. The ToR for the EIA should be summarized, explaining the reasons for any variation with them. A copy of the complete ToR should be appended where appropriate.

Description of the proposal and its alternatives: A description of the proposal and the alternatives indicates the elements and main activities that will take place during project construction, operation and decommissioning. This section of the report draws attention to the major differences between the alternatives, including the no-action alternative. It can also include information on:

- The project setting and the major on-site and off-site features (e.g. access roads, power and water supply, etc.);
- Resource use, raw material inputs and emission and waste discharges;
- Operational characteristics, processes and products;
- The relationship of the technical, economic, social and environmental features of the proposal; and
- Comparison of alternatives and options (such as size, location, technology, layout, energy sources, source of raw materials) within the above context.

The above information is given in only enough detail for impact prediction and mitigation measures to be understood and appreciated. Wherever appropriate, maps, flow diagrams and other visual aids are used to summarise information.

Description of the affected environment: A concise description is needed of the biophysical and socio-economic conditions of the affected environment. Baseline information should include any changes anticipated before the project begins. It should provide only the necessary background and baseline against which to understand impact predictions. Current land use and other proposed development activities within the project area should also be taken into account. This indicates how the proposal relates to current policies and plans and whether or not it is consistent with them.

Key aspects of the affected environment that need to be included for this purpose include:

- spatial and temporal boundaries;
- biophysical, land use and socio-economic conditions;
- major trends and anticipated future conditions should the proposal not go ahead; and
- environmentally-sensitive areas and valued resources that may need special protection.

Public consultation and inputs: A concise, yet complete, statement of the nature, scope and results of public consultation is an important section of the report. These particulars are sometimes overlooked or aspects are insufficiently described. The points to include depende on the provision made for public consultation in guidelines.

Environmental impacts and their evaluation: This section of the EIA report evaluates the potential positive and adverse impacts for both the proposal and its alternatives and for each component of the environment identified as important in the ToR. Impact characteristics are described as predictions of magnitude, severity, occurrence, duration, etc. The significance of residual impacts that cannot be mitigated should be explicitly stated.

Information contained in this section includes:

- prediction of each major impact, its characteristics and likely consequences;
- consideration of their compliance with environmental standards and policy objectives;
- recommended measures for avoiding, minimising and remedying the impact;
- evaluation of significance of the residual impacts (stating the standards or criteria used); and
- limitations associated with impact prediction and evaluation, as indicated by the assumptions made, gaps in knowledge and uncertainties encountered.

The section can also indicate how environmental data was gathered, the predictive methods used and the criteria used to judge significance. It is helpful to present information in summary form to give readers an overview of the impact characteristics of the proposal and the alternatives to it.

Comparative Evaluation of Alternatives and Identification of the Environmentally Preferred Option

In this section, the proposal and the alternatives are systematically compared in terms of adverse and beneficial impacts and effectiveness of mitigation measures. As far as possible, the trade-offs should be clarified and a clear basis for choice established. The environmentally preferred option should be identified and reasons given for the selection made.

Shortcomings Encountered in Preparing EIA Reports

An EIA report should be complete, easily understood, objective, factual and internally consistent. These objectives are difficult to achieve in a process that involves many contributors working to tight deadlines. Even so, far too many EIA reports fall short of meeting their basic purpose of providing the necessary and relevant information for decision-making and clearly communicating key findings to the public and other interested parties.

Higher standards could be achieved by addressing some of the shortcomings and deficiencies that are commonly found in EIA reports. The following sample list was compiled primarily from the experience of the Netherlands EIA Commission, which is an independent body responsible for the review of EIA reports.

Shortcomings and Deficiencies of EIA reports and Reporting Examples

Shortcoming	EIA Reporting Example
The objective and alternatives are too narrowly stated	An EIA report on a proposed by-pass road identifies the objective as relieving traffic congestion, failing to consider broader transport issues and alternatives.
The description of the proposal does not cover the key features	An EIA report describes the proposed construction of an industrial plant but omits information about construction of a pipeline and other facilities to transport and handle raw materials and finished products to and from the plant.
Key problems affected by the proposal are not described	An EIA report describes the proposed construction of a coal-fired power plant using surface water as cooling medium. It does not divulge that the surface water body is already used by other industrial activities for this purpose to the limit of its cooling capacity.
Sensitive elements in the affected environment are overlooked	An EIA report for a pipeline project does not indicate that the proposed alignment will dissect certain areas of ecological value.
Appropriate mitigating measures are not considered	An EIA report for a sanitary landfill does not describe a system for collecting methane gas produced in the landfill, even though greenhouse gas emissions contribute to climate warming and should be capped at current levels.
The alternative offering the best protection to the environment is not described or insufficiently described	An EIA report for a bridge or seabed tunnel across an estuary does not examine the alternative of a drilled tunnel underneath the estuary, which will have a much lower adverse impact on the environment.

Source: Netherlands EIA Commission

2.18. Guidelines for Effective EIA Report Preparation and Production

Usually, EIA reports are the product of a team of consultants and specialists. Most proposals have a number of different types of potential impacts (biophysical, socio-economic, health, etc) and their analysis requires a range of expertise. An EIA Project Manager or team leader has responsibility for forming an interdisciplinary team and managing its work.

The EIA report is a decision document, not a compendium of technical information. As such, the EIA report should be both rigorous and easily understood. It must effectively communicate the findings to the public at large, local people affected by the proposal and interest groups, as well as decision-makers who are the primary users.

Distribution of the report: Usually, EIA reports are available to the public and distributed widely. However, the institutional arrangements for this purpose differ. As a general guide, the EIA report should be accessible to all those who have an interest in, or are affected by, the proposal. Where public consultation has been extensive, it can be useful to lodge the EIA report in public institutions and distribute the summary to all individuals who have registered their names. Other measures may be needed in many developing countries, particularly where proposals directly affect poor and non-literate communities.

Other forms of presentation: Depending upon the circumstances, other forms of presentation of the findings should be considered.

These include:

- use of local media, radio and television;
- community report back;
- newsletters, information sheets;
- walk-in and storefront displays; and
- feedback through political representatives, local chiefs or other power structures, as appropriate.

Purpose and Elements of the EIA Review

The purpose of review is to examine and determine whether the EIA-report is an adequate assessment of the environmental effects and of sufficient relevance and quality for decision-making.

Key objectives of EIA review are to:

- assess the adequacy and quality of an EIA report;
- take account of public comment;
- determine if the information is sufficient for a final decision to be made; and
- identify, as necessary, the deficiencies that must be addressed before the report can be submitted.

In many EIA systems, the review stage is the major opportunity for public involvement. However, the arrangements for this purpose vary considerably from country to country. They range from notification of a period for receiving written comments on the EIA report to holding public hearings. Typically, the latter mechanism is part of an independent review by an EIA panel or inquiry body, which is considered to be a particularly transparent and rigorous approach.

An interim or prior review of EIA preparation can provide an informal check on the quality of work, to verify that is satisfactory and meets requirements. Normally, this will carried out by the responsible authority. However, the proponent can undertake an internal review of EIA quality as part of due diligence or quality assurance. In this way, proponents can ensure their work is of an appropriate standard before it is subject to external review. This can help to avoid delays associated with the issuance of deficiency statements or requests for additional information.

The elements of EIA review and the aspects considered differ with the arrangements that are in place in a particular country. A comprehensive review of the adequacy and quality of an EIA report would address many or all of the following issues:

- Does the report address the Terms of Reference?
- Is the necessary information provided for each major component of the EIA report?
- Is the information correct and technically sound?
- Have the views and concerns of affected and interested parties been taken into account?
- Is the statement of the key findings complete and satisfactory, e.g. for significant impacts, proposed mitigation measures, etc.?
- Is the information clearly presented and understandable by decision makers and the public?
- Is the information relevant and sufficient for the purpose of decision making and condition setting? The response to the last question is the most significant aspect for review conclusions, and will largely determine whether or not an EIA can be submitted as is or with minor revisions.

2.19. Procedure, Steps and Methods in the EIA Review

Most EIA systems provide for review of the EIA report. However, the procedures established for this purpose differ considerably, possibly more than for other process elements. The conduct of EIA reviews is based on both informal and formal arrangements. Marked variations exist in their particular requirements, forms of public consultation and the roles and responsibilities of lead agencies. An issue common to all EIA review procedures is how to ensure objectivity.

Specific procedures for EIA review that are in place in different countries are shown in the table below.

In general, these can be divided into two main types:

- *internal review (more informal)-* undertaken by the responsible authority or other government agency, with or without formal guidelines and procedure; and
- *external review (More formal)-* undertaken by an independent body, separate from and/or outside government agencies, with an open and transparent procedure for public comment.

Selected Examples of EIA Review Procedures

Project	Example
Environmental agency	Australia
Independent panel or mediator	Canada (only for major proposals)
Standing commission of independent experts	The Netherlands

Source: Scholten (1997)

Main Steps

There are a number of steps can help to achieve good practice in the review of EIA reports. First you need to establish a framework for the EIA review, including the following steps :

Set the scale/depth of the review: How much time is available to carry out the review? Are the necessary resources available for this purpose? The answers to these questions will depend mainly on the provision made for review within the EIA system and the Terms of Reference. The nature of the proposal will determine the speed and intensity of the review.

Select reviewer(s): The environmental issues and the technical aspects of the proposal will determine the expertise required by a review team or individual.

Use input from public involvement: Inputs from public involvement has proved to be important in checking and evaluating the quality of the EIA report; for example, with regard to the description of the affected environment and community, the attribution of significance of residual impacts, the effectiveness of mitigation measures and the selection of an alternative.

Identify review criteria and aspects to be considered: A systematic review will be based on specified criteria, for example, based on the ToR/available Guideline

Once you have established this framework for review, you will then need to undertake and report the review, which involves the following steps:

- carrying out the review;
- determine how to remedy any deficiencies; and
- report the findings.

The Review can be Carried out in Three Steps

- Step 1: identifies the deficiencies in the EIA report, using the Terms of Reference, relevant guidelines and criteria and information from any comparable EIA reports and their reviews.
- Step 2: focuses on any shortcomings in the EIA report and separate crucial deficiencies, which may directly impede decision-making, from less important ones. If no serious omissions are found, this should be stated clearly.
- Step 3: recommends how, and when, any serious shortcomings are to be remedied to facilitate informed decision-making and appropriate measures for project implementation.

2.20. EIA Review and the Acceptability of the Proposal

A range of methods can be used to review the adequacy of an EIA report. The methods are generally the same as those used in impact analysis and include:

General checklists: These can be adapted to review purposes, using compliance with local EIA legislation or guidelines as the starting point.

Project specific checklists and guidelines: These can be based on a general or sectoral checklist, with further adaptations to suit the requirements of the specific project and its terms of reference.

EIA review frameworks and packages: A number of these are available. The Environmental Statement Review Package developed by the EIA Centre, University of Manchester is widely referenced and used by non-specialists.

Expert and accredited reviewers: One or more experts can be used to peer review the adequacy of the report. The expert(s) contracted should be independent from those involved in preparing the EIA report. In some countries, including Ethiopia EIA experts are accredited or registered as capable of carrying out a study or review.

Public hearings: Public hearings, held by an independent EIA panel, commission or other inquiry body, on an EIA report give the highest level of quality assurance.

A structured and systematic process can be followed to test the quality of the report and to integrate technical evidence and public comment.

2.21. EIA Review Guideline of India

The following requirments Five hard copies and an electronic copy should be submitted to the relevant reviewing authority or agency as the case may be.

Reviewing conducted at various stages in the EA processes. *This include reviewing of* screening report; scoping report; Terms of Reference (TOR); Environmental impact assessment report, and Performance (monitoring or audit) reports at different stages in the project cycle.

Reviewing may Include Considerations of the Adequacy of

- Compliance with the "approved TOR",
- Required information,
- The examination of alternatives, assessment of impacts, appropriateness of mitigation measures and monitoring schemes as well as implementation arrangements,
- The use of scientific and analytical techniques,
- The extent of public involvement and reflection of IAPs concerns, and
- Presentation of the information to decision makers at Regional, Sectoral, and Local levels.

NB. Reviewing will be made based on reviewing guidelines prepared by EPA. For detail information and requirements consult this guideline.

Decision Making

At the end of this session, students are able to:

- Describe the role and contribution of EIA in the decision-making process, particularly the final approval of the proposal.
- Understand the broad trade-offs that must be made among environmental, economic and social factors in decision-making and condition setting.

The EIA process was introduced with the express intention of incorporating environmental considerations into decision-making on major proposals. All of those involved in EIA require an understanding of how the decision-making process operates and the particular contribution made by EIA.

Decision making is the process of choosing between alternative courses of action. When the term 'decision making' is used in EIA it is usually taken to mean the final approval. However, a number of inevitable 'interim' decisions will be made by several decision-makers for complex, or even relatively simple, projects throughout the EIA process. The number and type of the decision-makers will depend on the EIA procedures and legislation operating in the country of the project. Many decisions are made by the proponent (e.g. choices between various project alternatives). Some decisions may be made jointly by the proponent and the government (e.g. Screening and scoping decisions). The Table shown below illustrates the decision points in the EIA process.

Action	Decision-maker	Outcome(s)
Selection of project alternatives to be considered	Proponent	Preferred project alternative
Screening of project proposal	EIA agency/ regulator	No EIA; preliminary EIA; or, Full EIA required
Approval of scoping report or ToR.	Proponent and/or EIA agency/regulator	Approval of report and/or ToR
Review and acceptance of EIS	EIA agency/ regulator	Approval; approval with conditions; or, rejection of EIS
Consideration of EIS, review report, and other planning issues.	Planning authority and/or relevant Ministry	Approval of project (with conditions); or, rejection of project.

The final approval of the major proposal is normally a political decision, often taken by the national government, planning authority or other equivalent body. In some EIA system the approval is a pre-requisite to gaining other necessary authorizations, such as licenses and pernites, which are issued by regulatory agencies.

Role of the Decision-makers

Decision makers at all levels now have well understood environmental responsibilities. At a general level, these responsibilities are outlined in the Rio Declaration of Environment and Development and Agenda 21, the principle and program of action to which all countries that attended the Earth Summit are politically committed, including Ethiopia. However, some decision maker still regards EIA negatively, as an impression or impediment rather than as an opportunity to add value to development proposals and to safeguard critical resources and environmental functions. Meanwhile, UNEP, world Bank and other international organizations have warned that global environmental change may be reaching critical thresholds. It is important for decision-makers to be aware of their responsibility to implement the EIA process and use its results to better manage the environmental impacts and risks of a proposal. At a minimum, decision-makers need to understand:

- The basic concept and purpose of EIA (and SEA);
- EIA requirements, principles and guidelines that are applicable;
- The effectiveness of their implementation and the implications for decision-making;

- Limitations that may need to be placed on information and advice contained in an EIA report;

- How EIA process and practice measure up to internationally accepted standards and to those in place in comparable countries; and

- The issues associated with public consultation in decision-making, including third party and legal challenges to the authorisation of proposals subject to EIA.

The sustainability agenda places further obligations on decision-makers. In order to meet them, decision-makers need to have the requisite knowledge and tools to take fuller advantage of EIA as a sustainability instrument.

Decision-makers should be encouraged to:

- Implement the sustainability commitments made at Rio;

- Broaden their perspectives of the environment and its values;

- Better communicate information and reasons for decisions;

- Apply the precautionary principle when addressing the environmental impacts of development proposals;

- Look for improved ways of making trade-offs among environmental, economic and social factors;

- Adopt more open and participatory approaches to decision-making; and

Review the EIA process of a given proposal may involve a chain of decisions, culminating in a final approval of the proposal, including:

- screening - to decide if and at what level EIA should be applied;

- scoping - to identify the important issues and prepare terms of reference;

- impact analysis- focusing attention on the consideration and choice of alternatives;

- mitigation- to identify measures to avoid, minimise or compensate for impacts; and

- review- to determine the quality and adequacy of the EIA report as a basis for approval of the proposal.

At each stage, an implicit or explicit decision will be made on whether or not the proposal is acceptable and can be justified environmentally. In practice, this is invariably favourable, unless a proposal has a 'atal flaw' or proves highly controversial and unacceptable to a large majority of people. This process of decision-making is iterative, whereby the conclusions reached at each stage narrow down the choices to be made at the next one. It raises a number of issues about the difference EIA information actually makes to interim decision-making and final approval of proposals.

What aspects and issues apply to EIA decision-making locally? For example, consider:

- What type of precedent is set by each stage of decision-making for the next one?
- How do the range of options and considerations become narrowed?
- To what extent does momentum build up in favour of approval as the decision-making process continues?
- What are the circumstances and conditions under which a proposal might not be approved?
- Are the conditions established by the approval and authorisation of a proposal enforced during the implementation phase?

2.22. EIA as Part of the Decision-making Process

EIA is part of a larger process of decision-making to approve a major proposal. This process is shown in the figure below. It results in a political decision, which is based on information from a number of different sources and involves making a large number of trade-offs. A balance must be struck between the benefits and costs; their environmental, economic and social elements must be weighed, and uncertainties and arguments over the significance of risks and impacts must be addressed.

Technical criteria	Full EIA	EIA Review
Economic	Screening	Technical review
Environmental	Scoping	Public review
Socio-Economic etc.	Impact evaluation and prediction	Review report and recommendations
Facts	Preparing EIS	
Public involvement	**Decision-making**	**Other inputs**
Project stakeholders	Prioritising problems/actions	Policy
Public groups	Final assessment of all aspects	Economic
Local people and groups		Political etc.
Values		

The factors that will be important in the final approval of a proposal include:

- findings of significant impact contained in the EIA report;
- inputs from economic and social appraisals; and
- other external pressures or political inputs to decision-making.

Taking account of the EIA report: The information provided by EIA is based on technical analysis and public involvement. It is a synthesis of 'facts' and 'values'. How these components are reconciled and documented in the EIA report can have an important bearing on the potential contribution it makes to decision-making. The usefulness of the EIA report for decision-making also depends upon the use of good practice at previous stages in the EIA process. At a minimum, decision makers are expected to take account of the information from the EIA process in final approval and condition setting. With few exceptions, an EIA process does not lead to the rejection of a proposal even when there are findings of potentially significant impacts. However, the results of the EIA process usually have a considerable bearing on establishing terms and conditions for project implementation.

Relating EIA to other inputs: As the above figure shows, EIA is undertaken together with economic appraisal, engineering feasibility and other studies. Because of these other inputs, the decision that is made may not be the environmentally optimal choice. The environmental consequences of the proposal must be balanced against economic, social and other considerations. These trade-offs form the crux of decision-making, and, typically, environmental considerations carry less weight than economic factors in the approval of development proposals. In this regard, an important question, on which opinion varies, is whether EIA should be a strictly neutral or an advocacy process that argues the case for the environment. The predominant view is that the role of the EIA practitioner is to:

- provide a clear, objective statement of the environmental impacts and their mitigation;
- bring the feasible alternatives and the environmentally preferred option to the attention of decision-makers; and, more arguably
- give contestable advice on the environmental acceptability of the proposal (for example, whether it can be justified in the circumstances).

Other inputs: External inputs to the final decision on a proposal often occur through a wider representation of views and interests. These pressures vary from country to country and project to project. Many large-scale proposals are controversial and encompass a broad range of issues on which opinion can be sharply divided. They can become symbols of needed development or of environmental destruction or social injustice.

The so-called 'big dams' debate exemplifies this aspect of decision-making. The largest and most controversial schemes, represented by the Three Gorges (China) and Sardar Sarovar (India) schemes, have provoked international debate over the advisability of building them and the adequacy of the EIA process that was applied (refer the Sardar Sarovar Scheme and and review it to see if there are points of comparison with similar local project, if any)

A summary of Information considered important for decision-makers is given in the table below. It lists generic key aspects of EIA reports which decision-makers need to take into account when making final approvals and setting conditions for project implementation.

Information Considered Important for Decision-makers

Decision-making stage	Important information
Background	Project background and the most important environmental issues involved
Policy Context	Basic development issue/problem being addressed (e.g. flooding, water shortage, etc)
	The relationship to environmental policies and plans
Alternatives	Alternatives to the proposal (including the best practicable environmental option (BPEO) or equivalent designation)
Public involvement	Key public views
	Concerns of affected communities
	Areas of agreement and disagreement
Impact analysis	Costs and benefits
	Distribution of gains and losses
Mitigation and monitoring	Adequacy of proposal measures
Conclusion and recommendations	main economic benefits, significant environmental effects and proposed mitigation measures
	The extent to which the proposal conforms to principles of sustainable development
	Design and operational changes to improve the environmental acceptability of the project

Adapted from OECD/DAC (1994)

- Responsibility of the Decision-Makers

The responsibility of decision-makers to consider the findings and recommendations of an EIA report varies from one jurisdiction to another. Normally, there are limited qualifications placed on the discretion of the decision-maker to approve or reject a proposal. Depending on the arrangements in place, the decision-maker may have to:

- meet no further requirements;
- take account of information in the EIA report;
- provide written reasons for the decision; or
- act in accordance with recommendations of an EIA review body, unless these are explicitly overturned.

There can be a number of different outcomes from decision-making (almost similar with the Ethiopia'sGuideline):

- the proposal can be approved;
- the proposal can be approved with conditions;
- the proposal can be placed on hold pending further investigation;
- the proposal can be returned for revision and resubmission; and
- the proposal can be rejected outright.

A number of checks and balances are built into EIA processes to help ensure accountability and transparency. The procedural controls are important for quality assurance of the information contained in an EIA report. Unless these are in place, the decision-maker may not be in a position to make an informed choice.

In addition, leading EIA systems have established conventions and rules for decision-making, which provide a further check on accountability. Some or all of the following rules and conventions for decision-making are required to be considered are mentioned in the APA's EIS procedural Guideline of Ethiopia

- a summary of evaluation is made available to the public;
- reasons for decision and conditions of approval are made public;
- there is the right of appeal against decision;
- approval can be reversed or permit can be revoked on the advent of changing circumstances,
- approval of a proposal can not immune the proponent from being accountable of the occurrence of adverse significant impacts in the course of the implementation of the project, and

In addition, approval of an EIA report is only mark a simple agreement to the proposal. The culmination of the approval procedure will be the issuance of an Environmental Clearance Certificate upon the satisfactory trial operation phase.

Implementation and Follow-up

Key Objectives of EIA implementation and follow up

Key objectives of EIA implementation and follow up are to:

- confirm that the conditions of project approval are implemented satisfactorily;
- verify that impacts are within predicted or permitted limits;
- take action to manage unanticipated impacts or other unforeseen changes;

- ensure that environmental benefits are maximised through good practice; and
- learn from experience in order to improve EIA process and practice.

The main components and tools of EIA implementation and follow up include:

- surveillance and supervision- to oversee adherence to and implementation of the terms and conditions of project approval;
- effects or impact monitoring-to measure the environmental changes that can be attributed to project construction and/or operation and check the effectiveness of mitigation measures;
- compliance monitoring-to ensure that applicable regulatory standards and requirements are being met, e.g. for waste discharge and pollutant emissions;
- environmental auditing- to verify the implementation of terms and conditions, the accuracy of the EIA predictions, the effectiveness of mitigation measures, and the compliance with regulatory requirements and standards;
- ex-post evaluation-to review the effectiveness and performance of the EIA process as applied to a specific project; and
- post-project analysis- to evaluate the overall results of project development and to draw lessons for the future.

These components are variously defined and delineated in the institutional arrangements and procedures established for this purpose by different countries. However, their generic functions are reasonably well understood.

Key terms are described in the accompanying box, and reference is made to the different types of monitoring, auditing and evaluation that may be undertaken as part of EIA implementation and follow up.

A conceptual distinction can be drawn between the respective aims of impact management and review and feedback of experience. In practice, however, these control and learning functions are not clearly separable. Rather they form part of a continuum of implementation and follow up activities, which are concerned with optimising environmental protection through good practice at all stages of project development. This process, when integrated with other environmental management and review tools, can be extended over the whole life cycle of the project.

Terminology of EIA Implementation and Follow up

Term	Description
Surveillance and supervision	Surveillance of the implementation of EIA terms and conditions can be undertaken by regular or periodic site inspections to check on compliance, observe progress and discuss issues. Supervision implies a more intensive direction of the environmental performance of on-site activities, ensuring they are carried out in accordance with the environmental management plan and/or contract specifications.
Monitoring	Monitoring refers to the collection of data through a series of repetitive measurements of environmental parameters (or, more generally, to a process of systematic observation). The main types of EIA monitoring activities are: • Baseline monitoring- the measurement of environmental parameters during a pre-project period for the purpose of determining the range of variation of the system and establishing reference points against which changes can be measured. • Effects monitoring- the measurement of environmental parameters during project construction and implementation to detect changes which are attributable to the project. • Compliance monitoring- the periodic sampling or continuous measurement of environmental parameters to ensure that regulatory requirements and standards are being met.
Auditing	Auditing is a term borrowed from accounting to describe a systematic process of examining, documenting and verifying that EIA procedures and outcomes correspond to objectives and requirements. This process can be undertaken during and/or after project construction, and draws upon surveillance reports and monitoring data. The main types of EIA related audits are: • Implementation audits- to verify that EIA implementation met the conditions of project approval. • Impact audits- to determine the impact of the project and the accuracy of EIA predictions. • Compliance audits- to verify that project impacts complied with environmental standards and regulatory requirements. • Effectiveness or policy audits- to check the feasibility of mitigation measures and the consistency of EIA practice.
Evaluation	Ex-post evaluation involves a policy-oriented review of the effectiveness and performance of the EIA process. It is concerned with the overall 'balance sheet' of an EIA, looking at what it achieved, which aspects were influential, and how the process could be improved. The guiding concepts are: • Effectiveness- the extent to which the EIA process has achieved its purpose(s). Depending on how these are defined, an effectiveness review can be conducted against the terms of reference, the information provided to decision-makers or principles and criteria of EIA good practice • Performance- the success of the EIA process as measured by its outcomes and results, e.g. the environmental benefits achieved or the effectiveness of mitigation in avoiding or reducing impacts. Surveillance, monitoring and auditing data are necessary for this purpose.
Post project analysis	Usually, a post-project analysis is undertaken once the project has been constructed and is about to enter the operational phase. The term implies a focus on project specific EIA experience, e.g. in relation to dams, highways, waste disposal sites or power generation. In this context, post-project analysis can include aspects of effectiveness and performance review, using impact and mitigation data from surveillance, monitoring and auditing.

Sources: Au and Sanvicens (1997) and Sadler (1988, 1998).

2.23. Tools for Environmental Management and Performance Review

EIA implementation and follow up can occur throughout project construction and continue into the operational phase, becoming part of a larger process of environmental management and performance review. The tools for this purpose have developed rapidly. In particular, environmental management systems (EMS) are now widely used by industry and business to manage the impact of their activities on the environment. The ISO 14000 series provides a framework of EMS principles, guidance and procedure, including environmental auditing, performance review and life cycle assessment or analysis. In the table below, these are grouped according to their primary use and purpose.

Some of these tools are still under development, and their use and even terminology varies. Already, however, there is an increasing recognition of the benefits to be gained by linking EIA preparation and implementation to EMS design and development; for example, initially through the transfer of information and subsequently through the use of standardised procedures. Looking ahead, EIA and EMS can be combined with other tools to take an integrated approach to the total environmental impact of the project cycle, along the lines indicated in the table below.

Environmental Management and Performance Review Tools

Purpose	Examples of available tools
Internalising the environment in policy and planning	SEA, technology assessment, comparative risk assessment
Planning and designing environmentally sound projects	EIA, SIA, risk assessment, environmental benefit cost assessment
Environmental management of the impacts of an operating facility or business enterprise	EMS (ISO 14000 series), total quality environmental management (TQEM), industrial codes of practice
Eco-design of processes and products	Environmental design, life cycle assessment, cleaner production
Monitoring, audit, and evaluation of performance	Effects and compliance monitoring, site, energy, waste, health and safety audits, and benchmarking performance

Guiding principles for carrying out the process of EIA implementation and follow up include the following:

- the project should be carried out in accordance with the conditions of approval and the commitments made in the EIA report/EMP;
- surveillance and inspection should be a routine elements for this purpose;
- the scope of other follow up activities should be commensurate with the significance of the potential impacts; and
- monitoring, auditing and evaluation should be undertaken when
  - potential impacts are likely to be significant,
  - mitigation measures are untried or their outcome is uncertain, and/or
  - new aspects of EIA process and practice have been introduced.

A comprehensive approach to EIA implementation and follow up would include many or all of the following steps and elements:

- inspect and check the implementation of terms and conditions of project approval;
- review the environmental implications of any changes that are required;
- monitor the actual effects of project activities on the environment and the community;
- verify compliance with regulatory requirements and applicable standards or criteria;
- take action to reduce or rectify any unanticipated adverse impacts;
- adjust the EMP, project specifications and related schedules as necessary;
- audit the accuracy of the EIA predictions;
- evaluate the effectiveness of the mitigation measures; and
- provide feedback to improve EIA process and practice in the future.

EIA implementation and follow up can be time consuming and expensive, and not all projects warrant full attention. A disciplined approach should be taken to planning this phase of the EIA process. Surveillance to oversee EIA implementation and ensure compliance with conditions of approval and regulatory standards is usually the bare minimum requirement.

The scope of follow up should be determined early in the EIA process. A decision should be made as part of the screening and scoping process, when requirements are established for baseline studies and monitoring. In part, these decisions determine what can be done in EIA follow up, for example by establishing the information that will be available for effects monitoring and audit. Later, the scope of the EIA follow up programme can be refocused as more detailed information on potential impacts becomes available.

Monitoring

Monitoring is a cornerstone of EIA implementation and follow up. Other components are dependent on the scope and type of monitoring information that is provided. The primary aim of monitoring is to provide information that will aid impact management, and, secondarily, to achieve a better understanding of cause-effect relationships and to improve EIA prediction and mitigation methods. Both the immediate and long-term benefits from undertaking monitoring as part of EIA are widely recognised, although not always realised.

Monitoring is used to:

- establish baseline trends and conditions;
- measure the impacts that occur during project construction and operation;
- check their compliance with agreed conditions and standards;

- facilitate impact management, e.g. by warning of unanticipated impacts; and

- determine the accuracy of impact predictions and the effectiveness of mitigation measures.

A sound baseline is a critical reference point for the conduct of effects monitoring. In turn, effects monitoring establishes the basis for corrective action when actual impacts are unanticipated or worse than predicted. Compliance monitoring, carried out through repetitive or periodic measurement, also can be used for this purpose. This may suffice as a safety net for certain projects, for example, where the mitigation measures are well tried and known to be effective. However, compliance monitoring will trigger impact management only if regulatory standards or specified conditions are exceeded and, on its own, may be insufficient for large-scale, complex projects.

By themselves, compliance and effects monitoring permit only reactive impact management, since they detect violations or adverse changes after the fact. In this context, it is important to tie the results of both types of monitoring to predetermined actions (or emergency responses), which are triggered on a threshold basis. A more proactive, adaptive approach to impact management can be instituted by combining compliance or effects monitoring with supervision or regular inspection of site clearance, construction and mitigation activities. The use of the precautionary principle can facilitate early warning of emerging problems.

The collection of monitoring data is expensive. It needs to be targeted at the information necessary to manage the impacts that are significant or review the aspects of EIA practice that are of particular importance. These aspects should be identified as early as practicable in the EIA process to optimise the contribution of monitoring data to EIA implementation and follow up. Monitoring involves designing the programme, collecting and analysing the data, establishing their linkage to impact management, auditing and other components, and interpretation and reporting of data.

The following points need to be agreed as part of the EMP and conditions of project approval:

- major impacts to be monitored;

- objectives of monitoring and data requirements;

- arrangements for the conduct of monitoring;

- use of the information to be collected;

- response to unanticipated or greater than predicted impacts; and

- measures for public reporting and involvement.

Monitoring requirements should focus on the significant impacts predicted in the EIA report, taking account of:

- the environmental values to be safeguarded;
- the magnitude of each potential impact;
- the risk or probability of each impact occurring;
- the pathways and boundaries of each impact; and
- the confidence in the prediction of each impact.

Monitoring programmes need to be constantly reviewed to make sure that relevant information is being supplied, and to identify the time at which they can be stopped.

Each discipline has established methods for monitoring and data collection. For example, the design of a programme to monitor the impact of a large-scale project involving discharge of toxic waste or effluent into a water body may encompass different methods to measure change in water quality, food chains, fish reproduction, reduction in income from fisheries and its effect on the local community. Generally, monitoring to detect chemical and physical changes is more straightforward than for biological effects or ecological relationships.

The general approach to effects monitoring is to compare the pre- and post-project situation, measuring relevant environmental impacts against baseline conditions. A common issue in all situations is how to differentiate the change attributable to a project from the variability that characterises all biophysical or socio-economic systems. In the real world, as opposed to laboratory experiments, cause-effect relationships are difficult to separate from the interaction of other factors. Eliminating or correcting for these intervening variables is the key to the design and conduct of a scientifically defensible effects monitoring programme.

Typically, this problem is addressed by establishing impact and control monitoring stations. The impact or treatment site is selected to be a receptor of an emission, hazard, event or action from the project. An example would be a water sampling station downstream from an effluent discharge point. The control or reference site is located outside the impact zone, but chosen to be representative of the variability experienced by the impact site. 'With versus without' project comparisons then can be made to determine the change or impact that is attributable to the project.

Monitoring programmes result in time series data, which can be analysed by:

- assembling the data in tabular or graphic format;
- testing for variations that are statistically valid;

- determining rates and directions of change; and
- checking these are within expected levels and comply with standards (e.g. water quality).

Some relational changes, such as in chemical constituents in water, can be presented graphically. Longitudinal studies based on numerical data or photographic or descriptive records also provide relevant information on changes and trends. The figure below is an example of monitoring data. It depicts the variation in contaminant levels and their relation to seasonal precipitation, including the effect of an extreme event (drought) on sulphate concentration. Also shown are the independent checks made by the regulatory agency on a proponentâ€™s data.

Monitoring data needs to be interpreted and reported to a non-scientific audience, including decision makers, the affected community and the general public. This may be the responsibility of a regulatory body, monitoring team or multi-stakeholder group, established specifically to bring a broad understanding and a range of views to EIA implementation and follow up.

Appropriate guidance should be sought when developing an environmental monitoring programme. Typically, some or all of the following issues will be addressed:

- representative impact and reference sites;
- methods for sampling and collection of data;
- independent checks for quality control and assurance of data;
- basis for statistical interpretation and inference of impacts;
- protocols for the conduct of environmental auditing; and
- mechanisms for reporting data and responding to issues that are raised.

Some elements of an effective environmental monitoring programme are listed in the table below. The following steps can help to implement these elements:

- define the scope and objectives of monitoring for each impact;
- identify the sites for observation, measurement and sampling;
- select the key indicators for direct measurement or observation;
- determine the level of accuracy required in the data;
- consider how the data will be analysed in relation to baseline and other data;
- establish a system for recording, organising and reporting the data;
- specify thresholds of impact acceptability; and
- set requirements for management action if monitoring indicates these are exceeded.

2.24. Environmental Auditing

 Environmental auditing is a review process similar to that carried out in financial accounting. Both result in a statement of facts, which certifies that practice is (or is not) in accordance with standard procedure. In the case of environmental auditing, there is an added level of interpretation, focusing on the factors of performance. The concern is to identify how the aspects, processes or systems under review can be improved.

The main techniques for conducting an environmental audit are:

- examination of records and documentation relating to impacts, actions taken to manage them and aspects of performance;
- interviews with management and line staff to corroborate factual information and probe areas of concern; and
- site inspection to check that environmental measures and controls are operating as described and intended.

A distinction can be made between environmental audits conducted as part of EIA and EMS implementation, respectively. EIA related audits, typically, are ad hoc, project-by-project in approach and use non-standardised methodology. EMS audits, typically, are conducted in accordance with ISO 14001 guidance and procedures, and oriented toward continuous improvement in managing the environmental impacts of an organisation, site, process, product, supply chain or input-output balances. However, both EIA and EMS audits have objectives, elements of approach and information sources in common.

EIA audits are used to:

- identify the impacts of project implementation;
- verify whether or not the conditions of approval have been implemented;
- test the accuracy of impact predictions;
- check the effectiveness of mitigation measures; and
- improve compliance and performance of EIA practice.

EMS audits include:

- site audits- to examine all aspects of environmental management of a facility or operation;
- compliance audits- to ensure an organisation or development meets pertinent legal, regulatory and voluntary or self imposed standards such as emission limits, discharge permits and operating licenses; and

- sector or issue-specific audits- to consider key aspects of environmental management and performance, such as waste disposal, energy use, cleaner production, health and safety and supply chains.

Guidance on the conduct of EIA audits emphasises that a well-designed monitoring programme is an integral element of good practice. The 'before and after' data collected by baseline and effects monitoring lays down an audit 'trail', which allows key impacts to be tracked and statistically verified.

The case example in the table below, from Hong Kong, illustrates the results of an EIA audit of a major project. It emphasises both the use of monitoring and audit to remedy deficiencies in EIA implementation and the difficulties of gathering evidence to verify their cause.

When selecting projects for a full audit, international experience indicates that priority should be given to those:

- with a high level of environmental, social, economic or political impact and visibility;
- that can yield usable results within the existing technical and budgetary constraints; and/or
- most at risk from deficiencies in the EIA implementation and follow up system, such as limited surveillance capability or lack of authority to enforce mitigation measures.

The case example also underlines some of the difficulties commonly experienced in the conduct of EIA monitoring and audit, including:

- limited baseline information on variability and causal relationships;
- qualitative and non auditable impact predictions;
- late changes to project design and mitigation (thereby altering the basis on which predictions are made); and
- long lead times before certain trends and impacts can be identified, for example, large scale but infrequent impacts (such as oil spills) or low dose, repetitive effects (such as exposure to heavy metals).

Other more flexible, less data demanding approaches can be taken in cases where an auditable trail of monitoring data is unavailable or insufficient. For example, 'spot' audits concentrate on significant impacts or priority concerns about mitigation measures. These can be undertaken either as a series of 'rolling' audits or a post-project analysis. An impact-backwards methodology can be used to compare EIA prediction and mitigation with environmental effects and outcomes. Impacts are verified iteratively by consultation and field checks and traced backwards to EIA practice (comparable to an effectiveness or policy audit).

2.25. Evaluation of EIA Effectiveness and Performance

Ex-post evaluation of EIA effectiveness and performance can be undertaken at a number of levels. In this section, the emphasis is on a 'before and after' review of a specific EIA process, focusing on what was achieved and which elements of approach contributed to good environmental outcomes. This type of evaluation can be undertaken as an integral component of EIA implementation and follow up, for example to identify the results and lessons of the experience and feed them back into policy action. However, examples of this approach are limited, and fewer still are based on a systematic review of surveillance, monitoring and auditing data.

Other evaluations of aspects of EIA effectiveness and performance that can provide relevant information include:

- annual or periodic reports on the implementation and performance of EIA systems, e.g. three year review of World Bank experience;
- national and comparative reviews of the quality of EIA reports, e.g. as undertaken in Australia, Canada and the USA;
- reviews of the relationship of the EIA process and decision-making; and
- post-project analyses focusing on the results of EIA inputs and activities.

Despite recent progress, however, there is a lack of widely agreed frameworks for conducting reviews of EIA effectiveness and performance in the above areas. By contrast, in the EMS cycle, review and reporting are integral procedures for improving environmental performance. In leading companies, these are combined with monitoring, audit and other tools to address all impacts of their operations. A review of EIA effectiveness and performance can replicate this approach to document and disseminate the lessons of experience and build the knowledge base on project-specific impacts.

Typically, the responsibility for EIA implementation and follow up activities will be divided among different agencies and individuals.

For example:

- the competent authority usually oversees the implementation of the terms and conditions of approval;
- the proponent (often through sub-contractors) normally carries out the scheduled activities, such as site clearance and preparation, construction and environmental management;

- the environmental or regulatory agency usually inspects mitigation measures, reviews monitoring data and verifies compliance and effectiveness; and

- the public can have a formal role in environmental monitoring and audit, e.g. where a stakeholder or community review committee is in place. In other cases, there may be provision for public disclosure of monitoring and audit reports and opportunities for informal review and comment.

CHAPTER III

WATER QUALITY ASSESSMENT

3.1. Introduction

Water is essential to Human being, animals, and plants and without water life on earth would not exist. Humans need water not only for drinking but also for various other purposes like bathing, washing, cooking, industrial, agricultural, and recreational activities. Depending on climate and work load, the human body needs about 3-10 liters of water per day for normal functioning. Part of this water is derived from food. Much larger quantities are necessary when water is used for other purposes such as personal hygiene, cleaning of cooking utensils, laundry and house cleaning. Therefore adequate supply of potable water is necessary for proper health care and significant socio-economic development.

Pure water is a chemical compound containing two hydrogen atoms and one oxygen atom. However, water which is absolutely pure is not found in nature; even water vapor condensing in the air contains solids, dissolved salts, and dissolved gases. As condensed water falls, it sweeps up other materials from the air and becomes still more contaminated on reaching the ground, running over the surface and percolating through the various strata of the soil. Generally water in its natural cycle collects many impurities. Hence, natural waters require physical, chemical and biological treatment, depending on the nature of existing pollutants, before being supplied for domestic use.

The materials found in water may be divided into living organisms and solid or dissolved organic and inorganic. Not all of these are harmful, and some may even be desirable for health, esthetic, or technical reasons. Potable water is one that is safe to drink, pleasant in taste, and suitable for domestic purposes. A contaminated water or polluted water is one that contains suspended or dissolved materials which makes it unsuitable for its intended use.

The primary objective of water treatment is to produce water which is safe and appealing for human consumption. Thus water collected from best available sources will be subjected to pass through various physical and chemical processes and unit operations. This will ensure the production of water of good physical, chemical and biological quality, and free from unpleasant taste and odour and containing nothing which might be harmful to health.

All surface water and some groundwaters require treatment prior to consumption to ensure that they do not represent a health risk to the user. Health risks to consumers from poor quality water can be due to microbiological, chemical, or physical contamination. However, microbiological contamination is generally the most important to human health as this leads to infectious diseases which affect all populations groups, many of which may cause epidemics and can be fatal. Chemical contamination, with the exception of a few substances such as cyanide and nitrate, tends to represent a more long-term health risk. An example of this is nitrate which can cause methaemoglobinaemenia in babies. Substances in water which affect the clarity, colour or taste of water may make water objectionable to consumers. As many microorganisms are found associated with particles in water, physical contamination may also represent a health risk as it extends microbial survival.

Most treatment systems are designed to remove microbiological contamination and those physical constituents which affect the acceptability or promote microorganism survival – largely related to the suspended solids in the water. A disinfectant is nearly always included in treatment plants of any size. This is done for two main reasons: firstly it is added to inactivate any remaining bacteria as the final unit of treatment; and, more importantly, to provide a residual disinfectant which will kill any bacteria introduced during storage and/or distribution.

3.2. Water Contaminants

Disease Causing Organisms

Adequate and Safe drinking water is important in the control of many communicable diseases which may be transmitted by water includes diarrhoea, cholera, typhoid, paratyphoid fever, Trachoma, Typhus, amoebic and bacillary dysentery. Diseases associated with inadequate and unsafe water can take a number of forms. This may be grouped accordingly in Table 3.1. Organisms which cause infection disease are normally spread through the fecal and urinary discharge of sick persons and carriers. Protection of water supplies against these agents is thus normally a matter of preventing discharge of inadequately treated wastewater into the source and provision of appropriate treatment mechanisms.Water borne diseases are those carried by water that is contaminated with infecting agents from human or animal origin. When the water is drunk the infecting agents will be ingested and may cause disease. Control of such diseases calls for improving the quality of the water.

Table 3.1: Diseases Related to Deficiencies in Water Supply and/or Sanitation

Group	Diseases
Diseases transmitted by water (waterborne diseases)	Cholera, Typhoid, Bacillary dysentery, Giardiasis, e.t.c.
Diseases due to lack of water (water-washed diseases)	Trachoma, Ascariasis, Hookworm, Typhus, e.t.c.
Diseases caused by infecting agents spread by contact with or ingestion of water (Water-based diseases)	Biliharziosis, Schistosomiasis
Diseases transmitted by insects which live close to water (Water-Related Vectors)	Malaria, Sleeping sickness

However a great many microorganisms are found in water, most being of no health significance. Diseases due to lack of water tend to be a serious health hazard. When people use very little water, either because there is very little available or because it is too far away to be carried home in quantity, it may be impossible to maintain a reasonable personal hygiene. Skin or eye infections are thus allowed to develop, and intestinal infections can much more easily spread from one person to another. The prevention of water washed diseases depends on the availability of, and access to adequate supplies of safe water.

Inorganic Contaminants

Inorganic contaminants include both suspended and dissolved materials. Suspended materials are undesirable for esthetic reasons, but their primary effect on quality lies in their ability to shield microorganisms from disinfectant.Dissolved inorganic which have health effects includes aluminum, arsenic, barium, cadmium, chromium, fluoride, lead, mercury, nitrate, selenium, and silver. Table 3.2 summarizes the effect of some of these and other common water contaminants.

3.3. Other Common Constituents of Natural Water

All Natural waters contain some dissolved mineral matter. The commonly encountered cations are sodium, potassium, calcium, magnesium, iron, and manganese, which are associated with the anionic species bicarbonate, carbonate, sulfate, and chloride. These contaminants do not have chronic or toxic health impacts. In fact, People are so accustomed to these impurities that distilled water tastes flat and unpleasant.The divalent cations contribute to hardness, which is sometimes defined as the ability to neutralize soap. Iron and Manganese contribute to hardness, but their more important effect results from their oxidation and subsequent precipitation. This causes metallic taste and discolored water which stain clothes, cooking utensils, and plumbing fixtures.

Sulfate in association with magnesium and sodium can have a pronounced laxative effect on people who are not accustomed to water. Chloride in high concentration can contribute a salty taste to water and is sometimes an indication of sewage contamination, since the chloride concentration increases when water is used for domestic purposes.Bicarbonate and carbonate results from the dissolution of carbonate rocks and provide a very important buffer system in natural waters.Dissolved gases in water include all those to which it is exposed. Those which are commonly encountered are nitrogen, oxygen, carbon dioxide, hydrogen sulfide, and methane. Hydrogen sulfide has a disagreeable rotten egg odor in low concentration, is poisonous in high concentration and contributes to corrosion of metals and concrete. Carbon dioxide can contribute to dissolution of subsurface minerals and corrosion of metals. Oxygen can contribute to corrosion of metals under some conditions.

Table 3.2: Suspended and Dissolved Impurities of Water

Type	Constitutes	Effect
1. Suspended impurity	a) Bacteria	Some cause disease
	b) Algae, protozoa	Odour, Colour, and Turbidity
	c) Silts	Murkiness, or turbidity
2. Dissolved impurity	a) Salts	
	I. Calcium and Magnesium	
	- Bicarbonate	Alkalinity
	- Carbonate	Alkalinity, hardness
	- Sulfate	Hardness
	- chloride	Hardness, corrosion
	II. Sodium	
	- Bicarbonate	Alkalinity, softening effect
	- Carbonate	Alkalinity, softening effect
	- Sulfate	Foaming in boilers
	- Fluoride	Dental flurosis or mottled enamel
	- chloride	Taste
	b. Metal and compounds	
	- Iron oxide	Taste, red colour, corrosiveness, hardness
	- Manganese	Black or brown colour
	- Lead	Cumulative poisoning
	- Arsenic	Toxicity, poisoning
	- Barium	Toxic effect on heart, nerves
	- Cadmium	Toxic
	- Cyanide	Fatal
	- Boron	Affect central nervous system
	- Selenium	Highly toxic to animals, fish
	- Silver	Discolouration of skin, eyes
	- Nitrate	Blue baby conditions; infant poisoning, colour; acidity
	c. Gases	
	- Oxygen	Corrosiveness to metal
	- Carbon dioxide	Acidity, corrosiveness
	- Hydrogen sulphide	Odour, acidity, corrosiveness

3.4.   Examination of Water

To asses the level of contamination and type of treatment required, water require proper and reliable examinations and analytic measurements i.e. to plan and implement the type and extent of treatment,natural waters must be analyzed for physical, chemical and microbiological parameters. Even after appropriate treatment further examination and laboratory testing is required to confirm its suitability for different uses.

Sampling

Sampling is the first essential step in assessing the quality of water. To obtain an accurate representation of the composition and nature of a water, it is first essential to obtain a truly representative sample of the source. A representative sample that highlights the exact condition existing in water must be collected. After collection, the sample must be handled and preserved carefully to prevent any alteration in physical, chemical, and biological state. Accuracy and reliability of analytical results depend on the sample collection program. The time, location, type, and frequency of sample collection must be decided according to the source of water. Generally two types of samples are collected:

- Grab and
- Composite

A grab sample is one collected at a particular time and place. It represents the condition of the water at the time of sampling. Grab sampling is preferred when the composition of water is fairly constant i.e. not changing frequently. In addition to this grab sampling is required for certain tests that must be performed at the sampling site itself, e.g. chlorine residual, dissolved oxygen, temperature, toxic gas emission etc.A composite sample is a number of grab samples collected at definite intervals of time over a fixed period and mixed. This sample represents the average characteristic of water over that particular period of time. The composite sample is preferred in the following circumstances:

- When the average water conditions over a period of time is needed.
- Plant efficiencies are to be estimated.

A.Sample Handling and Preservation

Sample handling and preservations are the most important aspects of water analysis. Water samples are collected for a variety of purposes:

- To assess the degree of treatment.
- To evaluate performance of a treatment facility.

- To know extent of pollutions etc.

When a sample is collected, during transportation physical, chemical, and biological, changes may occur that can alter the sample composition and produce false results. To overcome this, the samples should be handled carefully and preserved if the analysis is to be performed in the laboratory, rather than at the site. The following precautions should be taken for appropriate sample handling:

- Sampling bottles and containers should be washed with nonphosphate detergent, rinsed thoroughly with running water and finally rinsed with distilled water.
- A narrow mouth sample bottle should be used if any gaseous element is to be analyzed in the sample.
- With characteristics which are likely to be unstable such as dissolved gases, oxidizable or reducible constituents, etc the analysis must be done carried out in the field or the sample must be suitably treated to fix the concentration of unstable materials.
- A wide- mouth sample bottle is used to collect a sample rich in oil or grease content. The wide mouth allows the technician to clean and wipe the interior of the container thoroughly.

As only a few parameters can be measured at site during collection, a preliminary treatment or preservation is essential in many cases. Changes in the composition of a sample with time can be retarded by storage at low temperature (4^0c) and the exclusion of light is also advisable. Physical preservation of samples by cooling i.e. by keeping the sampling container on ice during transportation is highly essential.

For microbiological examination of water the following care should be taken:

- Bacteriological sampling bottles must be sterilized in an autoclave at 121^0c for 15min before each use.
- The sample must not be exposed to light. It must be transported in an insulated container filled with ice.
- The time of sampling, transportation and estimation should be minimized as far as possible. The estimation should be performed with in 6h of sampling.

B.Equipments and Reagents

High quality laboratory glassware is essential for all analytical purposes. For general laboratory use, the most suitable material for glassware is borosilicate glass commercially known as Pyrex This material is resistant to all chemicals and can withstand temperatures. The most common glassware used in water testing laboratories are beakers, flasks, funnels, cylinders, burettes, pipettes, reagent bottle, test tubes, and culture tubes.Sampling bottles used for the collection of water samples should be of good quality glass or plastic and free from toxic substances. Stoppers, caps, plugs must be resistant to the effect of materials stored in the container. Pyrex class, stoppers, cork stoppers, rubber stoppers are the common types of stoppers.

3.5.   Physical Examination of Water

Physical parameters define those characteristics of water that respond to the sense of sight, touch, or smell. Suspended solids, Turbidity, color, taste, odour and temperature fall into this category.

A.Suspended Solids (SS)

Solids in water fall into one of the following categories

- Dissolved
- Colloidal
- suspended

Dissolved solids are truly in solution and pass through a filter. The solution consisting of the dissolved components and water is homogeneous forming a single phase. Colloidal solids are uniformly dispersed in solution but they form a solid phase that is distinct from the water phase. Suspended solids have also a separate phase from the solution. Some suspended solids are classified as settleable solids.

Solids suspended in water may consist of inorganic materials such as clay, silt and other soil constituents or organic materials such as plant fiber and biological solids. These materials are often natural contaminants resulting from the erosive action of water flowing over the surfaces. Discharge of domestic and industrial wastewaters can be also a source of suspended solids. Although some dissolved solids may be perceived by the physical sense, they fall more appropriately under the category of chemical parameters.

Suspended materials may be objectionable in water because:

- It is esthetically displeasing and provides adsorption sites for chemical and biological agents.
- Some suspended solids may be degraded biologically, resulting objectionable by products.
- Suspended organisms may include disease causing and toxic producing organisms.

There are several tests available for measuring solids. Most are gravimetric tests involving the mass of residues. The total solids test quantifies all the solids (suspended and dissolved) in the water. It is measured by evaporating a sample to dryness and weighing the residue. The total quantity of residue is expressed as mg/l. Residues refer to solid matter suspended or dissolved in water. It may include organic and inorganic materials like clay silt, minerals, metals, grease/oil, leaves and other plants and vegetation fibers. Most suspended solids can be removed from water by filtration. Thus the suspend fraction of the solids in water sample can be approximated by filtering the water. Depending on their size solid can be classified as coarse, fine, colloidal, and dissolved as shown below:

Sizes of Particles in Water

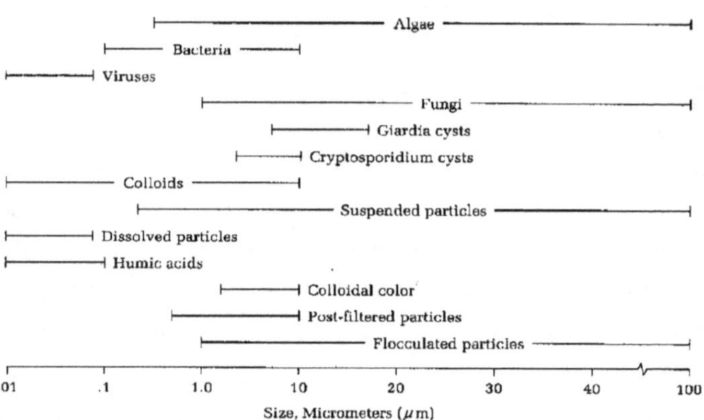

Turbidity: It can be simply defined as a measure of the presence of suspended solid materials in water. Or as a measure of the extent to which light is either absorbed or scattered by suspended material in water. Because absorption and scattering are influenced by both size and surface characteristics of the suspended material, turbidity is not a direct quantitative measurement of suspended solids. Turbidity results from the erosion of colloidal material such as clay, silt, or rock fragments, and metal oxides from the soil, vegetation fibers and microorganisms.

Turbidity has the following impact:

- Aesthetically turbid water is displeasing.
- Disinfection of turbid waters is difficult because of the adsorptive characteristics of some colloids and because the solids may partially shield organisms from the disinfection.

Turbidity is measured photomertically by determining the percentage of light of a given intensity that is either absorbed or scattered. The term nephelometry turbidity units (NTU) is often used to indicate the test was run according to the scattering principle. Turbidity meter reading can also be expressed as formazin turbidity unit, or FTUs.

Colour: Pure water is colorless but water in nature is often colored by foreign substances both in suspended and dissolved states. Colour imparted temporarily by suspended matter in water is called apparent color because it disappears on removal of suspended matter by filtration. Colour imparted permanently to water, which remains even after removal of suspended matter, is known as true colour. Hence, true colour is due to the presence of coloured dissolved solids in water.

Sources

- Organic materials like leaves, weeds etc.
- Inorganic materials like iron, and manganese.
- Discharge of industrial wastes e.g. from textile production, dyeing, pulp and paper, food processing, tanneries, mining, etc.

3.6.   Significance

Palatability and Suitability

Coloured water is not aestheticaly acceptable to the general public. Highly coloured water is unsuitable for laundering, dyeing, papermaking, beverage manufacturing, dairy production and other food processing, and textile and plastic production. Thus the colour of water affects its marketability for both domestic and industrial use.

Chlorine Demand

Colored water may exert a chlorine demand and reduce the disinfection power of chlorine when used in the treatment of water. While true colour is not usually considered unsanitary or unsafe, the organic compounds causing true colour may exert a chlorine demand and thereby seriously reduce the effectiveness of chlorine as a disinfectant.

Measurement

True colour of water can be measured by the Pt-Co method, which uses Potassium Chloriplatinate (K_2PtCl_6) as the standard. Colour comparison tubes containing a series of standards may be used for direct comparison of water samples that have been filtered to remove apparent colour. Results are expressed in true colour units (TCUs) where one unit of true colour of a centrifuged sample is equivalent to the colour produced by 1 mg/l of platinum in the form of chlorplatinate ions.

Taste and Odour: Odor and taste are two closely associated terms. Substances that produce an odour in water will almost invariably impart a taste as well. The converse is not true as there are many minerals known that impart bitter or salty taste to water without any contribution to odor production.

Sources

Many substances with which water comes into contact in nature or during human use may impart perceptible taste and odor. These include minerals, metals, and salts from the soil, end products from biological reactions, and constituents of wastewater.

3.7. Significance

Odor and taste are recognized as essential parameters influencing the palatability of drinking water, and the tainting of fish and other aquatic organisms and aesthetic of recreational water. Consumers find taste and odour aesthetically displeasing for obvious reasons. Such waters also pose a health threat because of the presence of decomposed organic constituents. Because water is thought of as tasteless and odourless, the consumer associates taste and odour with contamination and may prefer to use tasteless, odourless water that might actually pose more of a health threat.

Measurement

Measurement of taste and odor causing organics can be made using the Threshold Odor Number (TON) or Taste Threshold method.

Where A is the volume of odorous water

B is the volume of odour free water required to produce a 200ml mixture.

Temperature: The temperature of natural water systems responds to many factors, the ambient temperature being the most universal. Generally shallow water bodies are more affected by ambient temperature than deep water bodies. The temperature of surface waters governs to a large extent the biological species present and their rates of activity. Temperature has an effect on most chemical reactions that occur in natural water systems. Temperature has also a pronounced effect on the solubilities of gases in water. Temperature also affects other physical properties of water. The viscosity of water increases with decreasing temperature. The maximum density of water occurs at $4^{o}c$, and density decrease on either side of that temperature, a unique phenomenon among liquids.

3.8. Chemical Examination of Water

Water has been called the universal solvent and chemical parameters are related to the solvent capabilities of water. Examination of water in terms of its chemical constituents involves the determination of:

- Inorganic and Nonmetallic constituents which may include P^H, Alkalinity, Acidity, Hardness, Oxygen, Boron, Chloride, Cyanide, Fluoride, Silicate, sulfate.
- Metallic constituents such as Calcium, Magnesium, Iron, Sodium, Potassium.
- Nutrients like nitrogen and phosphorus.
- Organic Constituents e.g. BOD, and COD.

The source, significance and method of measurement for some chemical constituents of water are described below.

Total Dissolved Solids: The material remaining in the water after filtration for the suspended-solids analysis is dissolved solids. Like suspended materials dissolved substances may be organic or inorganic in nature. Many dissolved substances are undesirable in water. Dissolved minerals, gases, and organic constituents may produce aesthetically displeasing color, tastes, and odors. Some chemicals may be toxic, and some of the dissolved organic constituents have been shown to be carcinogenic. Not all dissolved substances are undesirable in water. For example, distilled water has a flat taste.A direct measurement of total dissolved solids can be made by evaporating to dryness a sample of water which has been filtered to remove the suspended solids. The remaining is weighed and represents the total dissolved solids (TDS) in the water. An approximate analysis for TDS is often made by determining the electrical conductivity of the water. The ability of water to conduct electricity, known as the specific conductance, is a function of its ionic strength. Specific conductance is measured by a conductivity meter and the result is expressed in millisiemens per meter (mS/m).

There is no a one-to-one basis of relation between specific conductance and concentration of TDS. Organic molecules and compounds that dissolve without ionizing are not measured. Additionally, the magnitude of the specific conductance is influenced by the valence of ions in solution, their mobility, and relative numbers. The temperature also has important effect, with specific conductance increasing as the water temperature increases. A multiplier constant ranging from 0.055-0.09 is used to convert millisiemens to mg/l. Because no distinction among the constituents is made, the TDS parameter is included in the analysis of water only as a gross measurement of the dissolved material. Thus, it is desirable to know more about the compositions of solids by making tests for several of the ionic constituents of the TDS. The ions usually accounting for the vast majority of TDS in natural waters are listed in Table below. Those listed under major constituents are often sufficient to characterize the dissolved solid content of the water. These are called common ions and are often measured individually and summed on an equivalent basis to represent the approximate TDS. As a check the sum of anions should equal the sum of cations because electro-neutrality must be preserved.

Table 3.3: Common Ions in Natural Water

Major constituents, 1.0-100mg/l	Secondary constituents 0.01-10.0mg/l
Sodium	Iron
Calcium	Strontium
Magnesium	Potassium
Sulfate	Carbonate
Chloride	Nitrate
Bicarbonate	Fluoride
	Boron
	Silica

P^H: P^H is a logarithmic scale generally used to express the acidic, alkaline, or neutral nature of solution. It represents the hydrogen ion concentration. Due to the hydrolysis of dissolved salts, the P^H value can decrease or increase beyond neutral value, i.e., 7.0, showing the presence of acid or alkali in the solution.P^H is an essential factor to be estimated in each and every phase of water. Because all the processes involved the treatment of potable water such as chemical coagulation, disinfection, softening, and corrosion control, are P^H dependant.The determination of P^H in water samples is based on determination of [H=] ion concentration by a potentiometer (P^H meter) using a glass electrodes with a reference electrode.

Alkalinity: Alkalinity is defined as the quantity of ions in water that will react to neutralize hydrogen ions. Alkalinity is thus a measure of the ability of water to neutralize acids. Alkalinity in water is mainly due to the presence of hydroxide (OH^-), carbonate (CO_3^{2-}), bicarbonate (HCO_3^-) of metals like Mg, Ca, and K. Phosphates, silicate ions and ammonia would also contribute alkalinity. These compounds result from the dissolution of mineral substances in the soil and atmosphere. They may also originate from the microbial decomposition of organic matter.

Sources

- **Atmosphere and soil:** The major constituents of alkalinity of natural water are bicarbonate (HCO_3^-), carbonate (CO_3^{2-}), and hydroxide (OH^-). These compounds result from the dissolution of mineral substances in the soil, and the atmosphere.

- **Industrial wastes:** Phosphates are mainly added from effluent of industrial wastes rich in soap and detergents. Fertilizers and pesticides present in agricultural wastes also contribute to phosphate alkalinity in water.
- **Biological sources:** H_2S and NH_3 are the major products of microbial decomposition of organic material containing sulfur and nitrogen under anaerobic environment. They may impart alkalinity to water.
- **Water softening:** If lime or lime-ash is used as a softening agent during chemical treatment of water, it increases the level of alkalinity.

3.9. Significance

In large quantity, alkalinity imparts a bitter taste to water. The principal objection to alkaline water, however, is the reactions that can occur between alkalinity and certain cations in the water will result precipitate that can foul pipes and other water-systems appurtenances. In order to design and operate a chemical treatment for the purification of water, alkalinity measurement is important to select the appropriate chemical for coagulation and softening of water.

Measurement

Alkalinity measurements are made by titrating the water with an acid and determining the hydrogen equivalent. Alkalinity is then expressed as milligrams per liter of $CaCO_3$.

Hardness: Hardness is defined as the presence of significant concentration of salts of multivalent metallic cathions mainly Ca^+ and Mg^+ ion's dissolved in water.Under supersaturated conditions, these cathions react with anions to form insoluble solids precipitates. Hardness is classified as carbonate hardness and noncarbonated hardness. Carbonate hardness is due to the presence of calcium and magnesium carbonate and bicarbonates in water. It is expressed in terms of $CaCO_3$ concentration in mg/l. Carbonate hardness is also known as temporary hardness because it is highly sensitive to heat and precipitates out readily on boiling. Noncarbonate hardness is due to the dissolution of salts of calcium other than carbonates and bicarbonates such as calcium sulfate $(CaSO_4)$ or calcium fluoride $(CaF2)$. This hardness is referred as permanent Hardness because it cannot be removed by boiling.

Sources

Hardness is water occurs due to the presence of multivalent metallic cations in like Ca^+, Mg^+, Fe^{2+}, Mn^{2+}, and Al^{3+}. The multivalent metallic ions most abundant in natural waters are calcium and magnesium others like iron, manganese, and aluminum are found in much smaller quantities. Therefore, for all practical purposes, hardness may be represented by the sum of the calcium and magnesium ions.

3.10. Significance

Hardness of water is an essential parameter in assessing the suitability of water for domestic and industrial uses for the following reasons.

- High soap consumption. Hard water does not produce lather or foam with soaps, hence results an economic loss to the water user.
- Hard water reduces the efficiency of boilers and heating systems in various industries due to the scale that is deposited on the equipment. This causes equipment breakdown and considerable economic loss.

Measurement

Hardness can be measured by using spectrophotometric techniques or chemical titration (EDTA titrimetric method) to determine the quantity of calcium and magnesium ions in a given sample. Hardness can be measured directly by titration with ethylene diamine tetra acetic acid (EDTA) using eriochrome black T (EBT) as an indicator. The EBT react with the divalent metallic cations, forming a complex that is red in color. The EDTA replaces the EBT in the complex, and when the replacement is complete, the solution changes from red to blue.Hardness may range from practically zero to several hundred, or even several thousand, parts per million. Although acceptable levels vary according to a consumer's feeling to hardness, a generally accepted classification is as follows:

$< 50\text{mg/l}$ as $CaCO_3$	Soft
$50\text{-}150\text{mg/l}$ as $CaCO_3$	Moderately hard
$150\text{-}300\text{mg/l}$ as $CaCO_3$	Hard
$>300\text{mg/l}$ as $CaCO_3$	Very hard

Dissolved Oxygen (DO): Oxygen is the most important element in water quality control. Its presence is essential to maintain the higher forms of biological life and the effect of waste discharge on a river is largely determined by the oxygen balance of the system. Clean surface waters are normally saturated with DO, but such DO can be removed rapidly by the oxygen demand of organic wastes. Oxygen saturated waters have a pleasant taste and waters lacking DO have an insipid taste; Drinking waters are thus aerated if necessary to ensure maximum DO. For boiler feed waters DO is undesirable because its presence increases the risk of corrosion.

Chloride: Chlorides are the common constituents of all natural waters. This may due to leaching of chloride containing rocks and soils, domestic sewage is also rich source of chloride human excreta, and mainly urine is rich in chlorides. Chlorides are not harmful or toxic to humans even at concentrations as high as 2,000mg/l. The higher concentration of chloride imparts an objectionable salty taste to water, which affects its palatability. The use of water containing high chloride content as cooling water boilers and other heating systems is restricted in industries. It affects the metallic pipes and related equipments. It can be measured by titration method.

Fluoride: Fluoride is seldom found in appreciable quantities in surface waters and appears in groundwater in only a few geographic regions (Like the central southern part of Ethiopia). Fluoride is toxic to humans and other animals in large quantities, while small concentrations can be beneficial. Concentrations of approximately 1.0mg/l in drinking water help to prevent dental cavities in children. However, excessive intakes of fluoride can result in discoloration of teeth. Noticeable discoloration, called mottling, is relatively common when fluoride concentrations in drinking water exceed 2.0mg/l. More than 5.0mg/l dosage of fluoride can also result in bone fluorosis and other skeletal abnormalities. It can be measured by colorimetric method.

Cyanide: Hydrocyanic acid and its salts represent the cyanide content in water. It is an important and commonly available industrial chemical. It can access water system via leakage of wastewater pipes or discharge of industrial wastes to surface waters. Cyanid and its compounds are highly toxic, especially at low PH, i.e., under acidic conditions. Cyanide ion has the ability to coordinate with the iron (Fe) atom in a hemoglobin molecule, and thus blocks the uptake of oxygen by the blood. Metallo-cyanide complexes formed by the reaction of CN- with heavy metals are extremely toxic in nature. Therefore, control of cyanide in industrial effluents is extremely important. It can be measured by titrimetric method.

Metals: All metals are soluble to some extent in water. Source of metals in natural waters include dissolution from natural deposits and discharge of domestic, industrial, or agricultural wastewaters. Metals are divided into Nontoxic metals and toxic metals, depending on their effect on human and other organisms. Nontoxic metals do not have health hazards. But excessive amount can impart other objectionable characteristics to water, such as taste, color, and hardness. Common metals included in this category are Ca, Mg, Na, Fe, Mn, Al, Cu, and Zn.Toxic metals are generally found in minute quantities and harmful to humans and other organisms. These metals falling under this categories are As, Cd, Pb, Cr, Hg, and Ag. Measurement of metals in water is usually made by atomic absorption spectrophotometer.

Nutrients: Nutrients are the elements essential for the growth, propagation and activity of plants, animals, even aquatic species, and microbes. A number of elements fall under this category, but the major elements are carbon, nitrogen, and phosphorus. Carbon is readily available from many sources. The major source is CO_2. This is available in abundance in the environment. Among nutrients, nitrogen and phosphorus are considered the limiting factors for the growth of plants and animals. The following Table summarizes the source, significance and methods of measurement of nutrients (N, and P).

Nutrients		
	Nitrogen	**Phosphorus**
Source	Environment Dead and decaying animals and plants Animal wastes, sewages, and industrial effluents Agricultural wastes	• Discharge of man generated wastes and runoff • Fertilizers, water treatment aids, detergents • Animal wastes, food residue and • Effluents of industries
Significance of examination	• High nitrogen content in water stream causes eutrophication. • An excessive amount of nitrates in potable water causes serious health hazards in infants.	• It stimulates the growth of algae and other aquatic plants • It interferes with the coagulation process in water treatment • It interferes with lime-soda softening of water
Method of Measurement	Titrimetric method and spectrophotometer method	Titrimetric method and spectrophotometer method

Organics: Many organic materials are soluble in water. Organics in natural water systems may come from natural sources or may result from human activities. Most natural organics consist of the decay products of organic solids, while synthetic organics are usually the result of wastewater discharges or agricultural practices. Dissolved organics in the form of starch, fats, proteins, alcohols, acid, aldehydes, cellulose, phenols and ester in water are usually divided into biodegradable and nonbiodegradable materials.Biodegradable materials consist of organics that can be utilized for food by naturally occurring microorganisms within a reasonable length of time. The amount of oxygen consumed during microbial utilization of organics is called the biochemical oxygen demand (BOD) The BOD is measured by determining the oxygen consumed from a sample placed in an air-tight container and kept in a controlled environment for a preselected period of time say five days. Measurement of the biodegradable organic matters is usually done by the biochemical oxygen demand (BOD). Measurement of the nonbiodegradable organic matters is usually done by the chemical oxygen demand (COD).

3.11. Bacteriological Examination of Water

Water may serve as a medium in which literally thousands of biological species spend part of their life cycle. From the perspective of human use and consumption, the most important biological organisms in water are pathogens, those organisms capable of infecting or transmitting disease to humans. These waterborne pathogens include species of bacteria, viruses, protozoa, and helminthes (parasitic worm).Analysis of water for all the known pathogens would be a very time consuming and expensive task. Because the number of pathogenic organisms present in polluted water are few and difficult to isolate and identify. Thus the purity of water is checked using indicator organisms. An indicator organism is one whose presence presumes that contamination has occurred and suggests the nature and extent of the contaminant.

Most of the waterborne pathogens are introduced through fecal contamination of water. Thus, any organism native to the intestinal tract of humans would be a good indicator organism. The intestinal track of human being contains countless rod-shaped bacteria known as coliform organisms. Each person discharges from 100 to 400 billion coliform organisms per day, in addition to other kinds of bacteria. Escherichia coli are found mostly in the intestinal tract of warm blooded animals and are exerted in large quantity with feces. Fecal coliform organisms are nonpathogenic and are believed to have a longer survival time outside the animal body than do most pathogens. Thus, coliform bacteria are usually used as indicators of the sanitary quality of drinking water. The presence of coliform bacteria is taken as an indication of that pathogenic organism may also be present, and the absence of coliform organisms is taken as an indication of that water is free from disease causing organisms.

However, the coliform bacteria include the Escherichia and Aerobacter and the use of coliforms as indicator organisms is complicated by the fact that there are other coliform groups which flourish outside the intestinal tract of animals. For example Aerobacter and certain Esherchia can grow in soil. These organisms are native to the soil and decaying vegetation and are often found in water that was in recent contact with these materials. Thus, the presence of coliforms does not always mean contamination with human wastes.

Because of the diverse survival characteristics and nature of exerted pathogens, a single perfect indicator for all pathogens is impossible. Hence, many organisms have been proposed as indicators of faecal contamination. These include; faecal coliform, faecal streptococci, Clostridium, Perfringens. A good indicator organism should possess the following properties:

- Be present exclusively in faeces and must always be present when there is the likelihood of pathogens being present.
- Occur in greater numbers than any pathogens in order to prevent their being diluted out in receiving water.
- Be easily isolated and enumerated.

- Show slightly greater resistance to survival in a water course than any pathogen, including resistance to chlorination and ozonation.
- Be non-pathogenic themselves to ensure that they do not pose a hazard to laboratory personnel.

The membrane filter method gives a direct count of coliform bacteria. In this test a portion of the sample is filtered through a membrane the pores of which do not exceed $0.45\mu m$. Bacteria are retained on the filter that is then placed on selective media to promote growth of coliform bacteria. The membrane and media are incubated at the appropriate temperature for 24h, allowing coliform bacteria to grow into visible colonies that are then counted. The results are reported in number of organisms per 100mL of water. An alternative method is the multiple tube fermentation tests.

3.12. Chemistry of Solutions

Important Terms

- Element: a fundamental substance that cannot be further decomposed by ordinary chemical means.
- Atoms: The smallest unit of each of the elements.
- Molecule: combination of atoms.
- Atomic mass: the number of protons in the atom.
- Atomic weight: the number o protons and neutrons contained in the atom.
- Molecular mass: the sum of the atomic mass of all the atoms in a molecule.
- Ions: the charged species are called ions, positive ions are called cations, and negative ions are called anions.
- Radicals: compounds with charges like CO_3^-
- Valence: number of charges on ions.
- Equivalence: absolute value of valance.
- A mole of an element or a compound is its molecular mass expressed in common mass units, usually, grams.
- Equivalent: Atomic mass or molecular mass divided by number of equivalence.

Examples

The atomic mass of hydrogen is 1 and the atomic mass of oxygen is 16. The molecular mass of hydrogen molecule is 2 and the molecular mass of water is 18. One mole of hydrogen is 2g and one mole of water is 18g. The valance of sodium is one and the equivalence of calcium is

2.The equivalence of an element or radical is defined as number of hydrogen atoms that element or radical can hold in combination or can replace in a reaction. In most cases the equivalence of an ion is the same as the absolute value of its valance. An equivalent of an element or radical is its gram molecular mass divided by its equivalence. Milliequivalent is the molecular mass expressed in milligrams divided by the equivalence and is often more use full in water chemistry because concentration of dissolved substances are more often in the milligram per liter range. Compounds are formed by combination of elements or radicals on a one-to-one equivalent basis. Equivalents are very important in water chemistry. Because in addition top being useful in calculating chemical quantities for desired reactions, it also provides a means of expressing various constituents of dissolved solids in common terms. An equivalent of one substance is chemically equal to an equivalent of any other substance. Therefore the concentration of substance A can be expressed as an equivalent concentration of substance B by the following method.

Expressed as B..................(i)

Dissolved constituents of water are mostly expressed as equivalent calcium carbonate concentration.

Examples

1.Tests for common dissolved ions are run on a sample of water and the results are shown below.

Constituents	
Cations	Anions
Ca^+ = 55mg/l	HCO_3^- = 250mg/l
Mg^{2+} = 18mg/l	SO_4^{2-} = 60mg/l
Na^+ = 98mg/l	Cl^- = 89mg/l

If 10% error is acceptable, should the analysis be considered complete?

Solution

First convert the concentrations of cations and anions from milligram per liter to milliequivalents per liter and sum them.

Ions	Cations		Anions		
	Conc mg/L	Concentration in meq/L	Conc. mg/L		Concentration in meq/L
Ca^+	55	2.75	HCO_3^-	250	4.10
Mg^{2+}	18	1.48	SO_4^{2-}	60	1.25
Na^+	98	4.26	Cl^-	89	2.51
Total		8.49	Total		7.86

Second calculate percentage of error:

Therefore accept the analysis.

What is the equivalent calcium carbonate concentration of:

a)   100mg/L of Nacl

b)   420mg/L $MgSO_4$

Solution

One equivalent of calcium carbonate is equal to 50mg/mequivalent.

One equivalent of sodium chloride is equal to 58.5mg/mequivalent

One equivalent of magnesium sulfate is equal to 60mg/mequivalent

By applying equation (*)

a)   of NaCl as $CaCO_3$

b)   of $MgSO_4$ as $CaCO_3$

How many grams of calcium will be required to combine with 90g of carbonate to form calcium carbonate?

Solution

One equivalent of calcium e is equal to 20g/equivalent.

One equivalent of calcium carbonate is equal to 50g/equivalent

One equivalent of carbonate is equal to 30g/equivalent

90g of carbonate is equal to 3 equivalent of carbonate.

To form the compound calcium carbonate the number of equivalents of calcium must be equal the number of equivalents of carbonate. Therefore, 3 equivalent of calcium which is equal to 60g is required to complete the reaction.

3.13. Water Quality Requirements

Water quality requirements vary according to the proposed use of the water. Water unsuitable for one use may be quite satisfactory for another and water may be deemed acceptable for a particular use if water of better quality is not available.Water quality requirements should not be confused with water quality standards. Water quality requirements represent a known or assumed need and are based on the prior experience of the water user. Water quality standards are set by a governmental agency and represent a statutory requirement. For example a farmer may know from prior experience that highly saline water will damage the crops, but there are no official water-quality standards that say such water cannot be used for irrigation purposes.

3.14. Potable Water Standards

Municipal water required for domestic uses, particularly the water required for drinking, must be colorless, odorless, and tasteless. It should be free from turbidity, and excessive or toxic chemical compounds. Harmless micro-organisms and radio activity must be absent. The quality of water for municipal supplies is, therefore, generally controlled throughout the world, and even World Health Organization (W.H.O) has laid down its international standards, specifying the minimum water quality requirements. When these water standards are not fulfilled, the water may not be 100 percent fit for drinking, and may be termed as "contaminated." Drinking water standards around the world are in a continuous state of evolution as more information becomes available and is evaluated. No single standard for drinking water quality suffices for all countries but there is a considerable degree of agreement on contaminants and their allowable concentrations.The world health organization has established minimum criteria for drinking water that all nations are urged to meet. These standards are listed in Table 1.4. Countries with more advanced technology generally have standards that exceed this quality.

3.15. Important Consideration in Setting National Drinking Water Quality Standards

The setting of drinking water quality standards requires careful consideration of a number of very important factors that must be observed. These include:

- Health Consideration
- Availability of water of better quality
- Aesthetic Consideration.

The primary aim of setting national drinking-water standards is the protection of public health and thus the elimination, or reduction to a minimum, of constituents of water that are known to be hazardous to the health of the community. However, standards achieve nothing unless they can be implemented and enforced, and this requires relatively expensive facilities and expertise as well as the appropriate legislative framework.The main reason for not promoting the adoption of international standards for drinking-water quality is the necessity of using a risk-benefit approach (qualitative or quantitative) to the establishment of national standards and regulations. This approach should lead to standards and regulations that can be readily implemented and enforced.

The establishment of drinking-water quality standards must follow a very careful process in which the health risk is considered alongside other factors, such as technical and economic feasibility. When establishing national standards, consideration must be given to the practical measures that will need to be taken with respect to finding new sources of water supply, instituting certain types of treatment, and providing for adequate surveillance and enforcement.National standards will, of necessity be influenced by national priorities and economic factors such as lack of resources for water treatment or unavailability of alternative water supply sources. Such economic factors, conflicting national priorities, and varying local geographical, dietary and industrial conditions may lead to national standards that differ appreciably from the WHO Guideline Values (GV).

Priorities for Setting Drinking-water Standards

- The first priority is to make sure that water is available to consumers, even if the quality is not entirely satisfactory. If there is a consideration to discontinue use of a contaminated water supply, there must be provisions made for instituting an alternative water supply.

- The second priority is to control the microbiological quality of the water supply. The consequences of contamination with pathogenic bacteria, viruses, protozoa and helminthes are such that their control must always be of paramount importance.

- Toxic chemicals in drinking-water must also be controlled if we are to prevent long term health effects from exposure to contaminants such as lead, arsenic or certain organic solvents.

- Finally, in assessing the quality of drinking-water, the consumer relies principally on the sense organs. Colour, taste, odour and appearance of the water, although not directly related to health, must be acceptable to the consumer. Some countries have elected to issue recommendations, rather than standards, for these aesthetic parameters.

CHAPTER IV

EIA IMPACT ANALYSIS AND MITIGATION MEASURES IN MINE AREA

4.1. The Purpose of the EIA

The environmental impact assessment (EIA) process is an interdisciplinary and multistep procedure to ensure that environmental considerations are included in decisions regarding projects that may impact the environment. Simply defined, the EIA process helps identify the possible environmental effects of a proposed activity and how those impacts can be mitigated. The purpose of the EIA process is to inform decision-makers and the public of the environmental consequences of implementing a proposed project. The EIA document itself is a technical tool that identifies, predicts, and analyzes impacts on the physical environment, as well as social, cultural, and health impacts. If the EIA process is successful, it identifies alternatives and mitigation measures to reduce the environmental impact of a proposed project. The EIA process also serves an important procedural role in the overall decision-making process by promoting transparency and public involvement. It is important to note that the EIA process does not guarantee that a project will be modified or rejected if the process reveals that there will be serious environmental impacts. In some countries, a decision-maker may, in fact, choose the most environmentally-harmful alternative, as long as the consequences are disclosed in the EIA. In other words, the EIA process ensures an informed decision, but not necessarily an environmentally beneficial decision.

4.2. Importance of EIA

When a project is proposed and design that project may affected the environment including impacts on air and water quality. economic disruption for a community or even impacts on social interaction. This possibility needs to be evaluated so that negative effects can be minimized or made up for some mitigation and measures. EIA documents that contain detail analysis of proposed project that may have environmental social and economic Impacts. They are required for major federal action some eia requires that can be predicted and environment quality of life for human and organisms.

4.3. Aim and Objectives

- The aims and objectives of EIA can be divided into two categories.
- The immediate aim of EIA is to inform the process of decision making by identifying the potentially significant environmental effects and risk of development proposals.

- The ultimate aim of EIA is to promote sustainable development by ensuring that development proposals do not undermine critical resources and ecological functions or the well being lifestyle and livelihood of the communities and peoples to depend on them.

- Improve the environment design of the proposal ensure that resources are used appropriately and efficiently identify appropriate measures and facilitate informed decision making including setting the environmental terms and conditions for implementing the proposal.

- Protect human health and safety avoid irreversible changes and serious damage to the environment safeguard valued resources, naturals areas and ecosystem components and enhance the social aspects of the proposal.

4.4. Benefits of the Study

- Potentially screens out environmentally-unsound projects
- Proposes modified designs to reduce environmental impacts
- Identifies feasible alternatives
- Predicts significant adverse impacts
- Identifies mitigation measures to reduce, offset, or eliminate major impacts
- Engages and informs potentially affected communities and individuals
- Influences decision-making and the development of terms and conditions

4.5. Description of the Environment

Study Area and its Environments

The study region is mainly of forest, barren land, wet and dry cultivable land and falls in zone II moderately stable in the seismic zonation map of India. The region does not have bird sanctuaries, biosphere reserves, national parks, breeding and green pastures, archaeological monuments and other sensitive area.

Environmental Methodology

The scope or study includes a detailed characterization of environment in an area of 10km radius of the mine site for environmental components based on the guidelines stipulated in EIA notification by MOEF.

- To assess the present status of air, noise, water, land, biological and socio-economic components of environment.

- To identify and quantify significant impacts of mining operations on environmental components.

- To evaluate the existing pollution control measures.To prepare an Environmental Management Plan (EMP) outlining the additional control strategies to be adopted for mitigation of adverse impacts.

- To delineate the post-mining environmental quality monitoring programme, to be followed by mines areas

4.6. General Approach To Environment

The Environmental besides data comprise of the features present of the site area its includes environmental features such as forest area, conservation area, water bodies, industries, wild life and fauna place of historic and importance etc.,

- Air pollution
- Noise pollution
- Vibration pollution
- Water pollution

Baseline data were collected on

- Ambient air quality monitoring
- Noise level monitoring
- Ground vibration monitoring
- Ground water quality monitoring

4.7. Meteorological Data

Meteorological data were collected in the mine site during the study period. The meteorological data on wind direction, wind velocity, ambient temperature and relative humidity were collected including maximum and minimum temperature, relative humidity and rainfall data are given below.

Table 4.1: Analysis of Meteorological Parameter Test Report

S.No	Parameters	Results			
1	Wind directions	SW	SW	SW	SW
2	Wind speed	3.01	2.89	2.65	2.13
3	Temperatures(min)	27.8	22.5	25.8	25.0
4	Temperatures(max)	39.7	40.5	39.3	36.7
5	Relative humidity(avg)	78.5	79.6	79.9	80.7

4.8.   Air Quality Monitoring

Air is the Earth's atmosphere. Air around us is a mixture of many gases and dust particles. It is the clear gas in which living things live and breathe. It has an indefinite shape and volume. It has no color or smell. It has mass and weight. Air creates atmospheric pressure. There is no air in the vacuum of the cosmos. Air is a mixture of about 78% nitrogen, 21% oxygen, 0.9% argon, 0.04% carbon dioxide, and very small amounts of other gases. There is an average of about 1% water vapour.

Air Pollution

Air pollution occurs in many forms but can generally be thought of as gaseous and particulate contaminants that are present in the earth's atmosphere.

Gaseous Pollutants

- Sulfur dioxide (SO_2)
- Nitrogen oxides (NOx)
- Ozone (O_3)
- Carbon monoxide (CO)
- Volatile Organic Compounds (VOC)
- Hydrogen sulfide (H_2S)
- Hydrogen fluoride (HF)

These pollutants are emitted from large stationary sources such as fossil fuel fired power plants, smelters, industrial boilers, petroleum refineries, and manufacturing facilities as well as from area and mobile sources. They are corrosive to various materials which causes damage to cultural resources, can cause injury to ecosystems and organisms, aggravate respiratory diseases, and reduce visibility.

Particulate Contaminants

Particulates come in both large and small or "fine" solid forms. Large particulates include substances such as dust, asbestos fibers, and lead. Fine particulates include sulfates (SO4) and nitrates (NO3). Important sources of particulates are power plants, smelters, mining operations, and automobiles. Asbestos and lead affect organisms, while sulfates and nitrates not only cause health problems, but also contribute to acid rain or acid deposition and a reduction in visibility. Particulate matter, a term sometimes used instead of particulates, refers to the mixture of solid particles and liquid droplets found in the air. Toxic air pollutants are a class of chemicals which may potentially cause health problems in a significant way. The sources of toxic air pollutants include power plants, industries, pesticide application, and contaminated windblown dust. Persistent toxic pollutants, such as mercury, are of particular concern because of their global mobility and ability to accumulate in the food chain. More research is needed to fully understand the fate and effects of mercury and the many other toxic pollutants.

4.9.   Sources of Air Pollution

- Point Source pollution and
- Non-Point-Source Pollution

Pollution is the introduction of contaminants into the environment. The contaminants may be spewed into the air, water or soil. They contaminate our natural resources. In this activity, we are concerned with distinguishing between various sources of pollution.

Point Source Pollution

Point source pollution results when the contaminants come from a single location. Examples of point source pollution in the air and water are given below.

Air - A certain factory is producing chemicals. As part of the manufacturing process, certain poisonous chemicals and toxic gases result, such as benzene. The chemical company permits these toxins to be released from the stack at the factory without treating them. The untreated, toxic chemicals are released directly into the air.

Water - A company has a new tank. This tank is being treated with a special chemical. After the tank is treated, the treatment chemicals are drained into a stream that runs hear the building where the company is. The chemicals are released directly into the stream water without being treated or decontaminated to make them safe.

Each of these examples illustrates point source pollution. In each of the examples, the contaminant is introduced directly into the environment at a single location. There are laws to prevent this type of abuse but people do it any because they do not want to spend money, or they do not want to take the time necessary, or both. Environmental authorities are concerned with locating and punishing violations of environmental protection regulations. And, even if laws are followed now, these types of practices occurred in the past before the laws were enacted and the pollutants are still around.

Non-Point-Source Pollution

Non-point-source pollution results when contaminants are introduced into the environment over a large, widespread area. Some examples follow.

Air - People drive cars. When a car is running, the engine produces a variety of chemical products including oxides of nitrogen (some of which are toxic) and molecules of unburned hydrocarbons from gasoline.Similar pollutants and soot result from burning and other combustion processes. Combustion of fuel is used for heating homes and buildings. Large trucks and buses with diesel engines contribute to smoke and hydrocarbons.

New federal standards approved in late 2000 call for changes in these vehicles over a five-year period. Once the changes are in place, it is expected that emissions from these vehicles will decrease.Burning of fuels with a high sulfur content also produces sulfur dioxide which enters the air. Sulfur dioxide reacts with water in the air to produce sulfurous acid which is a major component of acid rain.

Water - Acid rain from the air can enter the water cycle. The result is that it enters the environment. The acid is harmful to fish and other creatures in fresh-water lakes and streams.

4.10. Site & Parameter Selection

Site Selection

- Away from source and other interferences(inlet 15m away from source)
- Height of inlet >3m (preferably 3-10m)
- Double the height of nearly wall / obstructed
- Free flowing, well mixed
- Elevation angle <30(from inlet to top of building)
- Collocated samples should be 2m apart from site

Parameters

- Sensitive location (SO2 & NO2)
- Health impact stations (all pollutants)
- Population & exposure (all criteria pollutants)
- Downtown (accumulative 50m away traffic intersection)

4.11. Types of Air Quality Monitoring

There are two types of air quality monitoring in mines,

- Ambient Air Quality (AAQ)
- Personal Air Quality (PAQ)

Ambient Air

Ambient air is basically the natural state of air in the outdoor environment, and is what humans and animals breathe. Plants and other organisms need it for survival, too. The exact composition of this sort of air can vary from place to place depending on fixed things like elevation, as well as more flexible things like pollution and smog. Its content and quality are directly affected by the day-to-day activities of humans. In turn, ambient air quality has a direct effect on both public health and the welfare of the Earth's ecosystems.Mines areahas carried out air quality monitoring in and around the mine site for ambient air quality monitoring system as per Regulatory Guidelines. The parameters covered are SO2, NO2, PM_{10}, PM2.5, Pb. The air samples have been taken and analysed for one season.

Ambient Air Quality

Ambient air quality refers to the quality of outdoor air to which the public has access. Poor ambient air quality occurs when pollutants reach high enough concentrations to affect human health and/or the environment. Ambient air quality is typically measured near ground level, away from direct sources of pollution.

Field Instrument

Fig. 4.1: PM10 PM 2.5 Air Quality Monitoring Machine

Operation Procedure

For measurement of PM2.5 dust concentration following steps to be followed

- PTFE filter need to be conditioned in desiccation for about 16 hrs or more and weight of filter need to be recorded using digital balance accurate up to 0.00001mg (0.01mg).
- Take 4-5 reading of weight and record the stable weight.

- Weight filter must be immediately loaded in the filter cassette and transfer it in covered box.
- Record weight and number of the filter in note book.
- Put grease on all push fit pipe O-ring fitting of filter holder, WINS impactor and PM 10 impactor.
- Open the WINS impactor and put 37 mm glass microfiber filter and drop 1ml impactor oil on the filter so that is fully wet. Now close the WINS impactor.
- Open the filter holder (lower portion of WINS impactor) and carefully quickly put filter cassette with weighted filter in the slot and tightened the filter holder immediately.
- Fit WINS impactor and filter in DGM box using provided clamp.
- Now push pipe and PM 10 impactor on WINS impactor and tight the round clamp so that pipe is securely hold straight. Intel blue colour cap need to fitted at top of the PM 10 impactor.
- Recorded time totalizer reading.

4.12. Air Environment

Air environment is responsible for the health of human beings, animals, wild life and vegetation. Air pollutants emitted by project and non point source are transported dispersed or concentrated by meteorological and topographical conditions.The atmosphere is dynamic system which absolute range of solid, Liquid or gases from both Natural and Manmade source. There substances travel through the air disappear and reveal among themselves and also with other substances both physically and chemically which result in air pollution.

The limestone propose to mine is non toxic which does not emit any undesirable pollutants in the form of solid liquid or gas. The dust emitted during the transportation of vehicles the drilling will be carried out in wet condition to prevent dust into air and the haul roads will be periodically sprinkled with mist water spray to prevent dust into the atmosphere. The area in and around is quit fresh and the impact an air environment will always be under controlled and will be monitored. No processing or beneficiation is proposed except mining hence the impact an air will be controlled monitored and mitigated.The ambient air quality within the study area on both core and buffer zone forms the baseline information. The air quality monitoring points selected based on the Meteorological conditions, topography of the study area and likely impact boundary location of the ambient air quality monitoring stations was selected on the basis of wind pattern.The ambient Air quality monitoring stations are shown in the map. Four major pollutions were consideration significantly.

- Particle matter   -   PM
- Suspended Particle Matter   -   SPM
- Sulphur dioxide   - SO_2
- Nitrogen dioxide   - NO_2

Respectively the overall of emission we identified the direction of the wind in the majority observed time was predominantly south west to North East direction.

Table 4.2: Ambient Air Quality Test Result

S.No	Test Parameters	Unit	Protocol	Results	CPCB Standards
1	Particulate matter less than 10 micron size (PM_{10})	$\mu g/m^3$	IS 5182 Part 23-2006	42.2	100
2	Particulate matter less than 2.5 micro size ($PM_{2.5}$)	$\mu g/m^3$	IS 5182 part 4-1999 (Reaff 2010)	32.2	60
3	Sulphur dioxide SO_2	$\mu g/m^3$	IS 5182 part 2-2001 (Reaff 2006)	4.0	80
4	Nitrogen Dioxide NO_2	$\mu g/m^3$	IS 5182 Part 6-2006	5.2	80

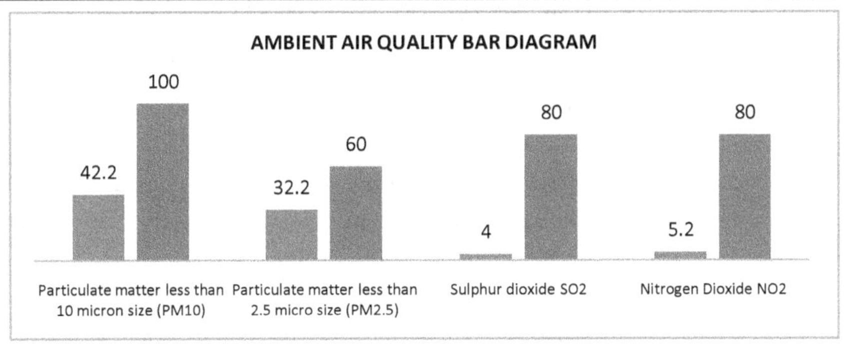

Personal Air Quality

Personal air quality refers to the quality of outdoor air to which the person has inhale. Poor personal air quality occurs when pollutants reach high enough concentrations to affect human health.

Table 4.3: Personal Air Quality Test Report

Si. No.	Test parameters	Test method	Unit	Results	CPCB LIMIT
1	Respirable Particulate Matter	Instrument Operating Procedure	$\mu g/m^3$	1.5	100

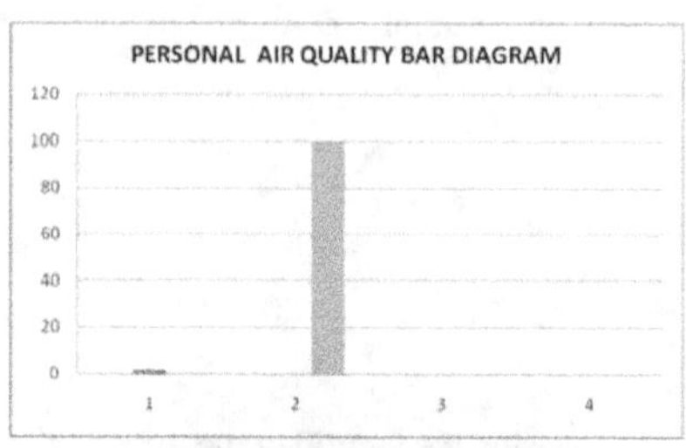

Fig. 4.2: Respirable Dust Sampler Noise Monitoring Instruments

Dust Emission

- Airborne emissions occur during each stage of the mine cycle, but especially during exploration, development, construction, and operational activities.

- Mining operations mobilize large amounts of material, and waste piles containing small size particles are easily dispersed by the wind. The largest sources of air pollution in mining operations are:

- Particulate matter transported by the wind as a result of excavations, blasting, transportation of materials, wind erosion (more frequent in open-pit mining), fugitive dust from tailings facilities, stockpiles, waste dumps, and haul roads. Exhaust emissions from mobile sources (cars, trucks, heavy equipment) raise these particulate levels.

- The blast holes are charged with slurry explosives. Hydraulic excavators are used to load the waste into dumpers.

- Blasting of rock, loading and transport of waste, drilling, these operations discharge dust into atmosphere of the mine air. The dust samples were collected and analysed.

Noxious Gases

- Gas emissions from the combustion of fuels in stationary and mobile sources, explosions, and mineral processing.
- During mining operation it is observed that the blasting operation, diesel machinery and dumpers play a major role in the emission of noxious gases in the mining area.
- The emission levels of sulphur dioxide (SO2), nitrogen dioxide (NO2), Particulate matter (PM10 & PM2.5), Lead (Pb).

Controling Factors

- Water sprinkling should be done prior and after loading into the trucks.
- In case of long transportation the trucks after loading should be covered with tarpaulin sheets to prevent spillage.
- Speed of the vehicles should be maintained within the prescribed limits.
- Trucks should not be over loaded and should be maintained to the body level and prescribed tonnage.

4.13. Noise Monitoring

Fig. 4.3: Noise Monitoring

Introduction

Noise is unwanted sound judged to be unpleasant, loud or disruptive to hearing. From a physics standpoint, noise is indistinguishable from sound, as both are vibrations through a medium, such as air or water. The difference arises when the brain receives and perceives a sound.

Sound is measured based on the amplitude and frequency of a sound wave. Noise is most commonly discussed in terms of decibels (dB), the measure of loudness, or intensity of a sound; this measurement describes the amplitude of a sound wave. On the other hand, pitch describes the frequency of a sound and is measured in hertz (Hz).

Sources of Noise Pollution

- The major noise generating source from the proposed activity is working machinery, jackhammer drilling, secondary blasting and plying of vehicles.
- Blasting is considered the major source environmental noise is the accumulation of all noise present in a specified environment.
- Noise pollution associated with mining may include noise from vehicle engines, loading and unloading of rock into steel dumpers, chutes, power generation, and other sources.
- Cumulative impacts of shoveling, ripping, drilling, blasting, transport, crushing, grinding, and stock-piling can significantly affect wildlife and nearby residents. Vibrations are associated with many types of equipment used in mining operations.

Types of Noise Monitoring

Generally Two types of noise monitoring conduct in mines,

- Ambient Noise Level Monitoring
- Work place noise monitoring

Ambient Noise Level Monitoring

In atmospheric sounding and noise pollution,ambient noise level (sometimes called background noise level, reference sound level, or room noise level) is the background sound pressure level at a given location, normally specified as a reference level to study a new intrusive sound source.

Ambient sound levels are often measured in order to map sound conditions over a spatial regime to understand their variation with locale. In this case the product of the investigation is a sound level contour map. Alternatively ambient noise levels may be measured to provide a reference point for analyzing an intrusive sound to a given environment. For example, sometimes aircraft noise is studied by measuring ambient sound without presence of any over flights, and then studying the noise addition by measurement or computer simulation of over flight events. Or roadway noise is measured as ambient sound, prior to introducing a hypothetical noise barrier intended to reduce that ambient noise level.

Ambient noise level is measured with a sound level meter. It is usually measured in relative to a reference pressure of 0.00002 Pa, *i.e.,* 20 µPa (micropascals) in SI units. A pascal is a newton per square meter. The centimeter-gram-second system of units, the reference sound pressure for measuring ambient noise level is 0.0002 dyn/cm^2. Most frequently ambient noise levels are measured using a frequency weighting filter, the most common being the A-weighting scale, such that resulting measurements are denoted dB(A), or decibels on the A-weighting scale.

Monitoring Method

The area is not inhabited by any wild life. Hence, there will not be any effect on migration of wild life from of area due to the noise created by the mining operations.Working shift is general which is between 9 a.m. to 5 p.m. No blasting operations are done in night. The effect of noise level generated by mining activity at various strategic areas was studied and the datas are tabulated.The area is not inhabited by any wild life. Hence, there will not be any effect on migration of wild life from of area due to the noise created by the mining operations. Working shift is general which is between 9 a.m. to 5 p.m. No blasting operations are done in night.

The noise level monitoring has been done in M/S Venketeswara Cements Ltd Minessite for one season. The details have been given.

Noise Environment

Sound/Noise can be defined as atmospheric or airborne vibration perceptible to the ear. Noise is usually unwanted or undesired sound. Sound loud enough to be harmful is called noise without regard to its other characteristics hence noise has a significant impact on the quality of life and in that sense it is a health problem in accordance with the (WHO) definition of health. Impact of noise on environment depends on various factors such as intensity distance from the source type of exposure and nature (Impulse or continuous), the type of activities movement of machineries, traffic density etc., hence it is to measure the levels so as to adjust the environment Impact and undertake amendment measures if warranted. Standard precession noise level meter were used for the purpose. The readings in the form of instantaneous sound measures levels were taken in the time brackets of two hours in order to here carry out assessment of noise level in the area.

There are no heavy industries nearby; the noise level of the area will be as same as the regional level. More over the noise level measurements does not rise for this area since very low explosives will be used for mining and the machineries to be used shall hydraulic types, it does not create much noise except the compressor, drilling and jet bummers. The traffic density in the area is very little. The average noise level in that area is less then 90dB (A) in and around 1Km radius. This noise level survey was carried out as per MOEF norms i.e., 1.5m above the ground level and 2mts away from the noise emit source. At present the noise is only through the movement of Vehicles in that area. No other significant noise emitting source found.

Table 4.4: Ambient Noise Level Monitoring Test Result

S.No	Location	Results dB (A)	CPCB Standard Limit
1	Project site – Centre area	41.2	70
2	Project Site SW corner	42.0	70
3	Project site SE Corner	41.4	70
4	Project site NE Corner	41.8	70

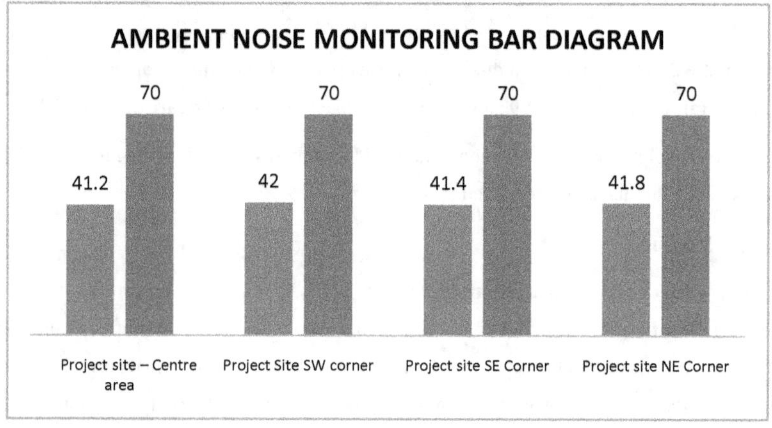

Work Place Noise Monitoring

Measuring noise levels and workers' noise exposures is the most important part of a workplace hearing conservation and noise control program. It helps identify work locations where there are noise problems, employees who may be affected, and where additional noise measurements need to be made.

Table 4.5: Work Place Noise Monitoring Test Result

Sl. No.	Location	Results dB (A)
1	Drilling area – 1	71.0
2	Drilling area - 2	79.8
3	Dozer machine operator cabin	71.6
4	JCB Operator cabin	76.8
5	Crane Operator cabin	73.5
*CPCB Limits		90 dB (A)

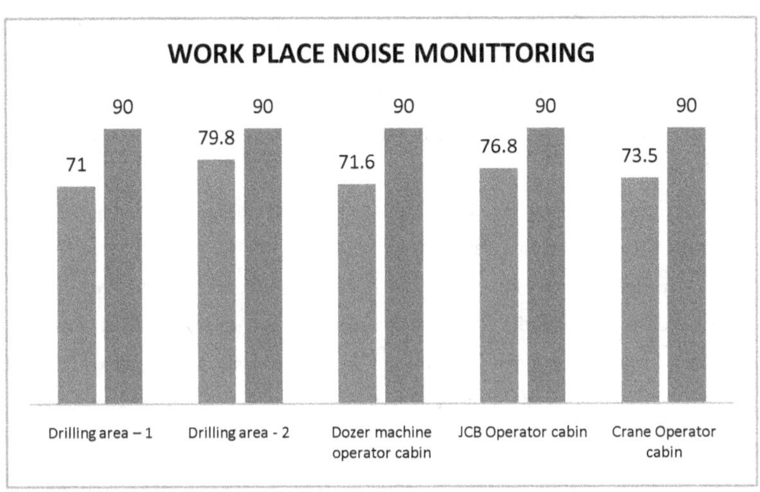

Impacts of Noise Pollution

- Noise pollution affects both health and behaviour.
- Unwanted sound (noise) can damage psychological health.
- Noise pollution can cause hypertension, high stress levels, tinnitus, sleep disturbances, and other harmful effects.
- These noise sources expose millions of people to noise pollution that creates not only annoyance, but also significant health consequences such as elevated incidence of hearing loss and cardiovascular disease.

Controlling Factors of Noise Pollution

There are a variety of noise controls available to reduce sound levels including source intensity reduction, land use planning strategies, noise barriers and sound baffles, time of day use regimens, vehicle operational controls and architectural acoustics design measures.

The following control measures are to be undertaken to bring down the noise levels.

- Proper maintenance of machinery, equipments and improvement on design of machines. Use of personal protective devices i.e., earmuffs and earplugs by workers, working in noise areas.
- Limited Blasting is proposed which will be carried out occasionally when only hard strata encounters.
- Limit the speed of haulage vehicles/tippers (below 20km)

- Thick plantation on the periphery of the mines.Proper gradient of haul roads to reduce cumulative noise levels.

- The green belt proposed will also help as acoustic barrier

- Creation of wide green belts of dense foliage between mine areas and residential villages.

- The greenbelt with species of rich canopy around the of area and along the roads will further attenuate the noise levels.

- It is proposed to the mine only eight hours a day from 9 a.m. to 5 p.m.Conducting periodical medical checkup of all workers for any noise related health problems

- Proper training to personnel to create awareness about adverse noise level effects.Planned noise monitoring at suitable locations in the project area and outside location for proper effective remedial actions.

- Displaying the noise level status of operational machines to enable control measures to be taken in this respect. This will enable to know the extent of noise level and to control the time to which the worker is exposed to higher noise levels.

Ground Vibrations is a technical term that is being used to describe mostly man-made vibrations of the ground, in contrast to natural vibrations of the Earth studied by seismology. For example, vibrations caused by explosions, construction works, railway and road transport, etc. - all belong to ground vibrations.Magnitudes of ground vibrations are usually described in terms of particle vibration velocity (in mm/s or m/s). Sometimes they are also described in decibels (relative to the reference particle velocity of 10^{-9} m/s). Typical values of ground vibration particle velocity associated with vehicles passing over traffic calming road humps are in the range of 0.1 – 2 mm/s. Magnitudes of ground vibrations that are considered to be able to cause structural damage to buildings are above 10–20 mm/s.

4.14. Vibration Monitoring Instruments

Fig. 4.4: Vibration Monitoring Instruments

Ground Vibrations is a technical term that is being used to describe mostly man-made vibrations of the ground, in contrast to natural vibrations of the Earth studied by seismology. For example, vibrations caused by explosions, construction works, railway and road transport, etc. -all belong to ground vibrations. Magnitudes of ground vibrations are usually described in terms of particle vibration velocity (in mm/s or m/s). Sometimes they are also described in decibels (relative to the reference particle velocity of 10^{-9} m/s). Typical values of ground vibration particle velocity associated with vehicles passing over traffic calming road humps are in the range of 0.1 – 2 mm/s. Magnitudes of ground vibrations that are considered to be able to cause structural damage to buildings are above 10–20 mm/s.

Vibration Monitoring Method

Monitoring stations at mines office, rest shelters in the mine site have been installed. For vibration datas two heavy blasts were conducted to study the parameters of Peak Particle Velocity (PPV) with different frequencies. This has been done in the season already decided.

Table 4.6: Ground Vibration Monitoring Test Report

S.No.	Time of Monitoring	11.00 a.m
1	Direction	North
2	Distance in meter	60 m
3	Bench Height in ft/m	4.5 m
4	Diameter of Hole in mm	40 mm
5	Depth of Hole in ft/m	6.0 mm
6	No.of Holes	13
7	Average Burden in ft/m	4 m
8	Type of Explosives	Slurry
9	Maximum Charge	15 kg
10	Peak per Velocity (PPV) mm/s	1.82 mm/s
Maximum Permissible Limit PPV, mm/s #		**15**

The vibration levels from the designed blasting pattern are expected to be well below the permissible limits, as the drilling and blasting will be carried- out with jack-hammer drills of 33 mm dia. The following mitigation measures shall be adopted.

Mitigation Measures for Vibration

- Peck particle velocity or ground vibrations for safety of nearby structures and residential building should be well within 12.5 mm/sec.
- To contain fly rocks, stemming column will not be less than the burden of the hole and the blasting area should be muffled.
- A danger-zone of 500 m from the blasting site shall be monitored.

- Charge weight used per hole will not exceed 300 gm

- Stemming column shall be more than the burden to avoid blow-out shots.

- Each blast shall be carefully planned, supervised, executed. Vibration has affected the stability of infrastructures, buildings, and homes.

- Blasting proposed will be carried out occasionally when hard strata encounters.

- During blasting, proper blasting pattern is adopted.

- The latest technology of delay blasting will be adopted to reduce the ground vibrations and noise generation during blasting operations.

- The following measures are proposed to contain the peak particle velocity due to blasting within the permissible limits based on operational experience and ground vibration studies carried out at the mine in the adjacent quarries.

- Sequential blasting machine will be used.

- Blasting will be done in only one bench at a time as the mineral ore body is not so hard, minimum blasting is sufficient.

4.15. Water Monitoring

Introduction

Water is a transparent and nearly colourless chemical substance that is the main constituent of Earth's streams, lakes, and oceans, and the fluids of most living organisms. Its chemical formula is H_2O, meaning that its molecule contains one oxygen and two hydrogen atoms, that are connected by covalent bonds. Water strictly refers to the liquid state of that substance that prevails at standard ambient temperature and pressure; but it often refers also to its solid state (ice) or its gaseous state steam or water vapour. It also occurs in nature as snow, glaciers, ice packsand icebergs, clouds, fog, dew, aquifers, and atmospheric humidity.

Water covers 71% of the earth's surface. It is vital for all known forms of life. On Earth, 96.5% of the planet's crust water is found in seas and oceans, 1.7% in groundwater, 1.7% in glaciers and the ice caps of Antarctica and Greenland. A small fraction in other large water bodies, and 0.001% in the air as vapor, clouds (formed of ice and liquid water suspended in air), and precipitation. Only 2.5% of this water is fresh water, and 98.8% of that water is in ice (excepting ice in clouds) and groundwater. Less than 0.3% of all freshwater is in rivers, lakes, and the atmosphere. Even smaller amount of the Earth's freshwater (0.003%) is contained within biological bodies and manufactured products.A greater quantity of water is found in the earth's interior.

Surface Water

Presently, the mining operation is spread all over the mining of area. The natural gradient is disturbed by excavation of mine activities. The contour plan of the area depicts that almost the entire quantity of the precipitated rainwater over the mining of flows towards south and northwest and in the buffer zone towards southwest.This area experiences good rainfall during monsoon period, proper channeling is done in mining benches to drain the water to the sump level which is at the bottom most point. Based on the above details it can be stated that the overall effect of mining on the surface water resources is very little.

The chemical analysis of the magnesite and groundwater do not show any toxic substances which can dissolve and pollute the surface water quality. The dust generated by drilling, blasting and loading operations get deposited and mixed with rainwater during the monsoon. They are carried as solid suspensions in water to the nearby nullahs.

Ground Water

It is observed that the ground water levels during monsoon period at 35m and 40m during summer below ground level. The mining operation is restricted well above the ground water level of the area without disturbing the same in the ML area and also the hydrological regime of the area in the buffer zones. The water consumption for the project is estimated to be 5 KLD. This quantity can easily be met with the existing ground water potential, safely.Water pollution is the contamination of water bodies (e.g. lakes, rivers, oceans, aquifers and groundwater). This form of environmental degradation occurs when pollutants are directly or indirectly discharged into water bodies without adequate treatment to remove harmful compounds.

Water Environment

Ground water occurrence in this area is about 35m depth below ground level. The mine operation will be carried out upto 28m below ground level; hence, the water level would not be affected by the mine operation. Water requirement is minimal in the proposed activity. The rain water shall be collected during monsoon and will be used for dust suppression and Afforestation.

Monitoring Arrangement

M/S Venketeswara Cements Ltd Mines has appointed an in-house Monitoring cell with qualified persons to monitor the data to be collected periodically at the monitoring stations of variouscategories described above.

Monitoring of Water Quality

Table 4.7: Water Quality Monitoring Test Report

Sl. No.	Test Parameters	Protocol	Unit	Results	WHO standard
1	Colour	IS 3025 Part 4 : (Reaffirmed 2012)	Hazen	<5	15
2	Odour	IS 3025 PART 5 : 1983 (Reaffirmed 2012)	-	Agreeable	3 Threshold
3	Turbidity	IS 3025 PART 10 :1984(Reaffirmed 2006)	NTU	2.7	5
4	pH @ 25oC	IS 3025 PART 2 :1983(Reaffirmed 2006)	-	7.0	9.2
5	Specific Conductance@ 25oC	IS 3025 PART 14 :1984(Reaffirmed 2006)	µS/cm	1098	
6	Total Dissolved Solids	IS 3025 PART 16 :1984(Reaffirmed 2006)	mg/l	810	1500
7	Total Hardness as $CaCO_3$	IS 3025 PART 21: 2009	mg/l	498	500
8	Calcium as Ca	IS 3025 PART 40 :1991(Reaffirmed 2009)	mg/l	180	200.0
9	Magnesium as Mg	IS 3025 PART 46 :1994(Reaffirmed 2009)	mg/l	132	150.0
10	Total Alkalinity as $CaCO_3$	IS 3025 PART 23 :1984 Reaffirmed 2009)	mg/l	440	500
11	Chloride as Cl^-	IS 3025 PART 32 :1988(Reaffirmed 2009)	mg/l	145	250.0
12	Sulphate as SO_4^-	IS 3025 PART 24:1986(Reaffirmed 2009)	mg/l	160	400.0
13	Iron as Fe	IS 3025 PART 53 :2003(Reaffirmed 2009)	mg/l	BDL(DL:0.1)	0.3
14	Zinc	IS 3025 PART 31 :1988(Reaffirmed 2009)	mg/l	3.4	5.0
15	Sodium	IS 3025 (Part 35) (RA 2003)	mg/l	169	200.0
16	Fluorides	IS 3025 PART 32 :1988(Reaffirmed 2009)	Mg/l	0.5	1.5

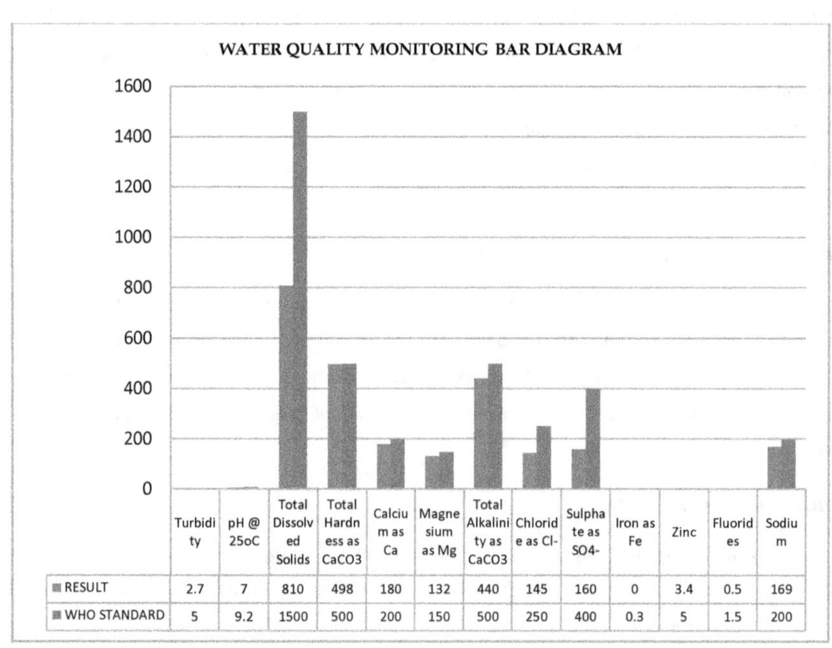

	Turbidity	pH @ 25oC	Total Dissolved Solids	Total Hardness as CaCO3	Calcium as Ca	Magnesium as Mg	Total Alkalinity as CaCO3	Chloride as Cl-	Sulphate as SO4-	Iron as Fe	Zinc	Fluorides	Sodium
RESULT	2.7	7	810	498	180	132	440	145	160	0	3.4	0.5	169
WHO STANDARD	5	9.2	1500	500	200	150	500	250	400	0.3	5	1.5	200

Mitigation Measures of Water Pollution

The chemical analysis of the iron ore does not show any toxic substance, which can dissolve and pollute water quality.

- Construction of parapet wall of appropriate dimension all along the toe of ore stock,
- Contour trench of appropriate width and depth all along the ore stock,
- Systematic drainage system for diverting the surface run-off during monsoon.
- Plantation of local varieties of species, so that there will be fast and healthy growth of vegetation.
- Regular monitoring and analyzing the quality of water.

4.16. Climate Conditions

The rain fall data of Ariyalur region in a year is 800mm. Temperature falls between 42°C in summer and falls down to 27°C in December-January. The wind direction is NE-SW and vice versa.

Flora and Fauna in and Around the Area

In small mining projects like this which involves very limited operations like secondary drilling and blasting, Conservation of Flora and Fauna along with ecology does not have significant impact of the overall eco system. A detail study related to flora and fauna was carefully observed physically by environmental engineers, Botanist and zoologist. The following table shows the flora and Fauna available at the region.

S.No	Common Name	Botanical name	Pictures
1.	Neem	*Azadirachata indica*	
2.	Ground nut	*Arachis hypogaea*	
3.	Coconut	*Cocos nucifera*	
4.	Millet	*Pennisetum glaucum*	
5.	Cotton	*Gossypium hirsutum*	
6.	Sugar cane	*Saccharum officinarum*	
7.	Gingelly	*Sesamum indicum*	

Fig. 4.5: List of Flora

Table. 4.8: List of Faunas

S.No	Common Name	Scientific name
1.	Goat	*Capra hircus*
2.	Rat	*Rattus norvegicus*
3.	Crow	*Corvus splenders*
4.	Squirrel	*Rodentia scrurus,*
5.	Ant	*Hymenopterous formicida,*
6.	Cat	*Felsis catus*
7.	Cow	*Bostaurus indicus*

4.17. Environmental Management Plan General

Environmental Management Plan (EMP) aims at the preservation of ecological system by considering in-built pollution abatement facilities at the proposed site. Some of the major criteria governing the environmental measures will be adopted, and the same is described in ensuing paragraphs.

Sustainable development in the project area needs to be intervened with judicious utilization of non-renewable resources of the project area and within the limits of permissible capacity. The assimilative capacity of the project area is the maximum amount of pollution load that can be discharged in the environment without affecting the designated use and is governed by dilution, dispersion and removal due to physio-chemical and biological processes.

The EMP is required to ensure sustainable development in the project area of 5 Km radius of the mine site under study; hence it needs to have a plan for encompassing the proposed activity. Government regulating agencies like Pollution Control Board working in the region and more importantly the people living in the project area need to extend their co-operation and contribution. It has been evaluated that the project area has not been affected adversely with the proposed activity and likely to get new economical fillip, not only for the project area but also for the region as a whole.

Mitigation measures at the source level and an overall management plan at the project area level are elicited so as to improve the supportive capacity of the receiving bodies. The EMP aims at controlling pollution at the source level to the possible extent with the available and affordable technology followed by treatment before they are discharged. Dust suppression in the haul roads to prevent dust emission.

4.18. Objective

- The main objective of the green belt is to provide a barrier between the mine and the surrounding areas.
- The green belt helps to capture the fugitive emissions and to attenuate the noise generated in the mine site apart from improving the aesthetics of the mine site.
- In order to control the industrial pollutants, dense tree plantations are necessary.

Environmental management for the proposed mine activity is discussed for the environmental impact pertains to the operational phase. Even though reversible in nature - all the impacts will be visible only during operational phase. It is planned to take corrective measures to ensure that these effects are kept to bare minimum. The EMP will therefore, be initiated during planning stage itself.

4.19. Economy

The present mining activity in this of area observed, does not make any adverse changes to the traditional way of life on the habitants in the nearby villages. The employees are mostly from surrounding villages. During the rainy season the local community depends upon the agricultural activity (no mining operation will be carried out in the rainy season). During the non-rainy season the villagers will be deployed for mining activity. Around 105 labours will be directly benefitted and indirectly around 200 will be benefited. Due to the mining activity many shops, restaurants, hotels, mechanical shops will sprung up which will give indirect employment to the villagers. Besides, the nearby remote villages will also be benefited by the shops, hotels, medical shops etc.

4.20. Environmental Policy/Legislation

Environment clearance of development projects including mining is done by the Government, with the following objectives:optimal utilization of finite natural resources through use of better technologies and management packages, and increasing suitable remedial measures at the project formulation stage.

The Policy Statement of Pollution issued by the Ministry of Environment and Forests Govt. of India in 1992, provides instruments in the form of legislation and regulation, fiscal incentives, voluntary agreements, educational programmers and information campaigns in order to prevent, control and reduce environmental pollution. The establishment and functioning of any industry including mining will be governed by the following environmental acts/regulations besides the local zoning and land use laws of the States and Union Territories.

- The Water (Prevention and Control of Pollution) Act, 1974 as amended from time to time (Water Act)

- The Water (Prevention and Control of Pollution) Cess Act, 1977, as amended (Water Cess Act)

- The Air (Prevention and Control of Pollution) Act, 1981 as amended (Air Act

- The Environment (Protection) Act, 1986 (EPA)

- The Wildlife (Protection) Act, 1972 as amended

- The Forest (Conservation) Act, 1980 as amended

- The Public Liability Insurance Act, 1991

- The Mines and Minerals (Regulation and Development) Act, 1957, as amended (MMRD Act)

- Circulars issued by the Director-General Mines Safety (DGMS).

Once the mining industry has been set up during the process of its life cycle, it is required to meet the standards of emissions, effluents and noise levels besides the compliance of other environmental acts/regulations including mining safety regulations. There also exists Guidelines for Integrating Environmental Concerns with Exploitation of Mineral Resources which identify some of the vital aspects relevant to environmental protection. These guidelines highlight the salient aspects of the various problems and briefly indicate some of the steps that need to be incorporated during the planning and various stages of the mining operations. The need for evolving certain tolerance standards/limits by the appropriate agencies has also been emphasized.

4.21. Mining Technology - Alternatives

Mining projects are site specific and location of the proposed mine is restricted to the geology and mineral deposits in the area. Geological, engineering and technical constraints determine the mining methods to be employed. The various alternatives/options available to mine the mineral are alternative mine locations. (this is mainly limited by geological parameters)

4.22. Assessment of Infrastructure Demand (Physical & Social)

Physical Infrastructure

- The existing road facilities are already available which shall be used and maintained.

- The labors requirement is drawn from the nearest villages. The labors will be brought by jeeps and vans to the mine site.

- Medical facilities are available near the project site, Government and private hospitals and other basic amenities and infrastructure facilities like communication center, school supermarket, bus stand are also available in Ariyalur at a distance of 7kms (NW).
- This mining project will provide employment for about 50 persons directly.

Social Infrastructure

- Periodical Medical checkup program for all the workers and first- aid fox with necessary equipment will be provided.
- Training for workers regarding occupational hazards.
- Safety equipment like dust mask, shoes, gloves, helmet etc.,

Venkateswara limestone mine has provided various facilities like outpatient dispensary, rest shelter, drinking water and transportation to its employees to their homes. Power linkage, water supply, communication facilities are the additional infrastructural arrangements which augments the socio-economic status of the villagers residing nearby. First Aid facility First-aid room has been provided as permanent structures within the of area applied for renewal. Labour Health Periodical medical checkup is being carried out as per directorate of mine safety norms, by a qualified Doctor.

Precautionary Safety Measures to the Laborers

Labours will be provided by

- Helmets
- Safety goggles
- Respiratory mask – ear plugs
- Refectory jackets
- Hand gloves as per the directorate of mine safety norms
- Mine boots
- No child labour is employed for any part of mining operation.
- All the labours, supervisors and managers are insured as per the Government norms.

Industrial Waste Management

No industrial waste will be generated from the project.

Drinking Water Management (Source & Supply of water)

This proposed mining project does not require huge water either for beneficiation or processing. Water requirement for mining activity is 1.0KLD. Water required for drinking and domestic consumption for labors is around 0.2KLD. The Packaged drinking water will be brought from approved water vendors nearby village. The domestic waste water generated will be sent to septic tanks followed by soak pits.

4.23. Waste & Sub-Grade Mineral Management

There is no sub grade mineral. The anticipated waste during the present period is about 1866069 Ts (94% waste). The mined waste is proposed to dump on the western side of the area on the existing mineral spoil dump (temporary dump). The dump mining and dump waste management will be discussed in the ensuing period after carrying out the exploration as per the UNFC norms.

There is an adequate space in the existing mine, hence the generation of waste during the present period will be dumped on the existing dump within the mine of area. As there is no non-mineralized zone within the mining of area the dump will act only as a temporary waste dump. When any part of the mine reaches the ultimate pit limit the same will be backfilled and mining will be programmed in the waste dump area. The waste will cleared out in the ensuing is period.The waste does not consist any toxic substance in the form of solid, liquid and gas. The waste is only the contamination of secondary minerals in the Magnesite mineral which cannot be separated.

Waste Management

The waste material is proposed to be dumped along the western side of the area as temporary dump. The waste dump will be stabilized by construction of retaining wall with waste lumps on slopes of the dump to prevent erosion, sliding and any danger from the dump. There is no chance for generation of toxic and hazardous element from this mine.

Top Soil Management

The topsoil is black cotton soil in nature. It occurs to a depth of 1m and it is being stored in the eastern boundary barrier and will be used for plantation purposes. The dimension of the existing topsoil dump is 160m x 5m x1m(h). There is no generation of topsoil during the present scheme period as most of the topsoil has been removed during the previous plan period.

Disposal of Mining Machinery

All the Machinery is at good condition. Moreover the machineries mostly are hired and used and hence, disposal of machineries do not arise.

4.24. Disaster Management and Risk Assessment

Necessary steps and measures will promptly be followed by the management at the time of any disaster or risk apprehended. There are no records of seismic activity, Landslides or Earth quakes in this project area. It is a high stable land situated in the stabilized strata of peninsular India.

Water Resource Management

It is an ongoing project. The water runoff used to flow naturally and used to join the nearby drainage nallah. It is proposed to collect and hold this runoff water and use it for various purposes within the area as explained in previous sections. The implementation of the project will not cause any alteration to the drainage pattern of the area. The quality of the water shall be maintained in compliance with the general effluent standards / drinking water standards.

Sanitary Installations

After being emptied, the decommissioned septic tanks will be removed or completely filled with gravel, sand, earth or inert material or shall be handed over to local authority who shall take further responsibility. Sewage sludge from treatment ponds will be used as manure in plantation area.

Green Belt Development

Fig. 4.6: Greenbelt Development in Mines

7.5m safety distance on the western boundary side is selected for Green belt development by planting and maintaining native species of Neem saplings. It is proposed to plant 50 plants per year. The total area for the proposed for Green belt is around **0.10.0Ha** out of 7.10.0Ha.

Green belt has been recommended as one of the major component of EMP, which will improve ecology, environment and quality of the surroundings of the mine site through:

- mitigation of fugitive emissions
- attenuation of noise levels
- waste water reuse
- development of ecosystem
- creation of an aesthetic environment
- Use of waste land to improve environmental quality.

The plant species with potential absorption capacity will be planted along boundary of the mine area for absorbing the air borne dust generated while mining. Suitable saplings as recommended by the in-house environmental cell of the company such as Pungan tree (Pongamaeapinnata) will be planted all around the mining area and garland drains will be created in the periphery of the mining area to prevent soil erosion. The company makes every effort to plant the saplings. About 0.10.0 Ha as proposed for afforestation at the earmarked location during the first five year mining period. At the end of the life of the mine about 0.40.0 Ha would be covered as Green belt development.

4.25. Design of Green Belt

A 7.5m wide greenbelt will be provided with trees planted in rows at a distance of 1m interval would be maintained.

- Plant Species for Greenbelt While selecting the plant species for the proposed green belt, the following points shall be taken into consideration:
- Should be a fast growing type;
- Should have a thick canopy cover;
- Should be perennially green;
- Should be preferably of native origin; and
- Should have a large leaf area index.
- Criteria for Selection of Species to be selected should fulfil the following specific requirements of the areas:
- Availability of seed material;
- Tolerance to specific conditions or alternatively wide adaptability to eco-physiological conditions;
- Rapid growth;
- Capacity to endure water stress and climatic extremes after initial establishment;

- Differences in height, growth habits and hollow types;
- Pleasing appearance;
- Capacity to selectively concentrate some materials from the surroundings;
- Providing shades;
- Providing for bio-mass and fodder and firewood;
- Ability of fixing atmospheric Nitrogen; and
- Improving waste lands.
- Some Additional Information About Plantation

To undertake plantation on site for different purposes, following steps will be involved:

- Raising seedlings in nursery;
- Preparation of pits and preparing them for transfer of seedlings; and
- After-care i.e. nurturing the sapling for proper growth
- Recommended Species for Plantation

The recommended plants for greenbelt are presented.

Mine Closure Plan

- It is an existing Limestone mine project.
- After the exploitation of Limestone mine reaches its ultimate pit limit, the pit will be partially backfilled and partially act as a good storage of water.
- Before closure the mine, a parapet wall will be constructed to prevent inadvertent entry of cattle and human beings.
- After closure of mine, the pit will be allowed to collect seepage and rain water. This will help to charge the nearby agricultural wells.

Mitigation Measure to be Undertaken for Safety and Restoration

- Drilling will be carrying out by wet drilling to control the dust into the air.
- Minimum blasting will be carrying out on limited scale.
- Mist spray on haul road will be proposed to prevent the dust propagation into the air.
- The plantation will be carried out on the safety barriers to prevent Noise, besides wet drilling will be practiced to prevent dust.
- All the machineries will be maintained in good conditions as per RTO and TNPCB Norms to prevent Noise, Smoke and vibration.
- Machineries will be periodically maintained by experienced mechanic to minimize noise, Smoke and ground vibration.

Recommended Plants for Greenbelt

Fig. 4.7: Newly Planted Work

Recommended Plants for Greenbelt

Table 4.9: Recommended Plants for Greenbelt

Plant species for mine area and its boundary	Plant species for road side and avenue boundary
1.Syzygiumcumminii	12.Syzygiumcumminii
2.Azadirachtaindica	13.Mangiferaindica
3.Polyalthialongifolira	14.Pithocolobiumdulce
4.Bauhinia purpuria	15.Tamarindusindica
5.Peltophorumferrusinium	16.Cordiadichotoma
6.Mangiferaindica	17.Delonixregia
7.Tectonagrandis	18.Delonixelata
8.Ficusreligiosa	19.Zizhhuphuszuzuba
9.Somaniasaman	20. Zizhuphusmauritiana
10.Bambusa multiplex	
11.Tamarindusindica	
Plant species for vacant places *Syzygiumcumminii,Peltophorumferrusinum,Terminaliaarjun, Tectonagrandis,Casiafistula,Bambueamultiplex,Tamarindusindica, Bauhinia purpuria, Bauhiniarecemosa, Sesbaniagrandiflora, Mangiferaindica.*	

The green belt plan at the post mining stage is shown in conceptual plan which is effective plan of mining.

4.26. Post Plantation Care

Fig. 4.8: Post Plantation Care

Investment on reclamation would be futile without adequate and timely aftercare. After care includes weeding, soil working, mulching and fertilizing, and if possible, irrigation to promote better growth of the planted seedlings. The vegetated area should be protected from grazing and browsing of animals until the plants are above the level of damage. Wherever necessary, fencing should be erected on the boundaries of areas.

Implementation of the project which is an existing mine provides opportunity for the people living nearby and there is chance for auxiliary industries like repair workshops, canteen, medical and transport facilities to the people employed from nearby villages. Moreover the management of the project takes care of nearby villages in respect of their socio-economic aspects. All the adverse effects caused by the mining operation in this project mentioned have been mitigated by taking suitable steps then and there and implementing them effectively.

4.27. Precautionary Care

The base line studies relents no hazardous levels of dust and noise and prevailing at theproject area. A well implemented environmental Management plan as discussed in the miningplan will help in mitigation the adverse effects due to quarrying activities.The project is a small operation were limited activities are being carried on the noisecreating device will be only jack hammer drilling which will always be mitigated in wetcondition to prevent noise and dust in the air. The movement of vehicles is very minimal. Theentire vehicle used will be periodically maintained by well experienced mechanic and kept under TNPCB standards, emission testing will be carried out periodically and water will be sprinkledperiodically to prevent dust into air. The small quantity of non humus rich surface soil will beremoved and preserved in the boundary barrier to facilitate the Afforestation.Blasting will be used for heaving effect and not shattering effect, hence the fly rockproblem will not arise. This is because the granite industry requires only huge blocks which arefree from induced cracks and fissures. The flora in the area is only small bushes as much of thearea is flat terrain. No trees are proposed to uproot for the project and Infect Trees will beplanted on boundary barrier which will act as acoustic sound barriers. Environmental care andattitude of preventing environment is inducted to the proponent and advice to carry out andmitigate the minor impacts due to quarrying. Appropriate persons are advice to get employed toprotect the Environment and Ecology of the area.

4.28. Management Plan and Suggestion

The environmental impact analysis has revealed hazardous levels of dust and noise prevailing at the various work spots in the mine. Implementation of environmental management plan has helped to reduce the dust and noise levels below the undesirable limits. Reduction of noise at source, interruption of noise in its path of propagation and protection of the receiver from high noise levels has further improved the working environment. Ground vibration was well within the limits at the time of EIA since proper blasting practices were being used. The humus-rich surface soil, scraped and removed from the surface, prior to opening of new pits, is conserved and is used for developing green belts on spoil dumps. As EIA and EMP have been made statutory requirements for starting new mining ventures as well as for existing mines, (at the time of renewal of mining plans) measures to prevent environmental degradation have become a subject of priority with the mine managements. Sequential Blasting Machine and Nonel Shock Tube Detonators would make it possible to exploit some of the rich mineral deposits which could not be mined otherwise due to environmental concerns. Apart from controlling the environmental degradation in the mine the EIA and EMP have helped to improve the life of lots of people inhabiting nearby villages.

Implementation of the project which is an existing mine provides opportunity for the people living nearby and there is chance for auxiliary industries like repair workshops, canteen, medical and transport facilities to the people employed from nearby villages. Moreover the management of the project takes care of nearby villages in respect of their socio-economic aspects.All the adverse effects caused by the mining operation in this project mentioned have been mitigated by taking suitable steps then and there and implementing them effectively.

As EIA and EMP have been made statutory requirements for starting new mining ventures as well as for existing mines, (at the time of renewal of mining plans) measures to prevent environmental degradation have become a subject of priority with the mine managements. Apart from controlling the environmental degradation in the mine the EIA and EMP have helped to improve the life of lots of people inhabiting nearby villages.

CHAPTER V

SOILS, GEOLOGY AND GEOMORPHOLOGY

5.1. Introduction

Much has been written about the links between soils, geology and civilisation, but considerably less is known about the impact of human activity on soils and geology. The EU/UK EIA legislation (see §1.3) specifically identifies soil as one of the main environmental *receptors* of development impacts for which assessments must be carried out. The DoE (1989) guidance on the scope of EIAs includes soil, agricultural quality, geology and geomorphology as topics in the checklist that should be included in an EIA. This has recently (June 2006) been updated by DCLG through a consultation paper *Environmental impact assessment: a guide to good practice and procedures*, (DCLG 2006a).

Soil is defined as the top layer of the land surface within the biosphere. It is a component/ subsystem of terrestrial ecosystems, providing a growing medium for flora, and a habit at for fauna. From the human perspective, soil is also the basis of agricultural and forestry production for food, wood, and textiles. Avoiding significant development impacts on the soil ultimately protects the whole of the ecosystem from degradation. An understanding of the local environment would be incomplete without reference to the underlying geology, but less emphasis is generally given to impacts on this, because relatively few types of development have significant impacts on geology. This chapter therefore concentrates on the assessment of significant soil impacts, although some important geological and geomorphological aspects are described briefly.

5.2. Definitions and Concepts–Geology and Geomorphology

Geology

Geology is a vast and complex subject, and only a few aspects of relevance to EIA will be mentioned here. Keller (2000) is a good introduction to environmental geology covering the topics of interest in this context. Surface geology concerns superficial deposits (e.g. drift, glacial deposits, river gravel) while solid geology only concerns pre-superficial formations. The three main groups of rock are igneous, sedimentary and metamorphic. Many different igneous rocks have formed as a result of volcanic activity, they are characteristically hard and crystalline,and have crystallised from magma, a silicate melt. Sedimentary rocks are formed from pre-existing rocks by processes of denudation and sedimentation.

They are relatively soft and easily eroded and include limestones, coal, evaporates and sedimentary iron ores. Sedimentary rock strata are often important as a quifers, and many are rich in fossils. Metamorphic rocks are formed as the result of heat, pressure and chemical activity on pre-existing solid rock. A number of aspects of geology are of direct importance in EIA. Earth Heritage Sites or Geological Conservation Review (GCR) sites (some of which are Sites of Special Scientific Interest–SSSIs) are important for the conservation, protection and management of their fossils, stratigraphy, minerals or other geological interest. They have scientific and amenity value, and include exposures of value to wildlife (e.g. rocky shores, shingle structures, cliffs, screes, and limestone pavements). The underlying geology also has engineering and construction implications, and affects both geochemistry, and geophysics (Ellison and Smith 1998, Bell 2000).

Some geological aspects are of less direct importance in EIA. For example, both the storage and movement of ground and surface waters, and water geochemistry will be affected by the hard geology of an area (see Chapter 10). In addition, the physical and chemical properties of soils will be determined, as mostsoils are derived from bedrock or transported rock. The geology and hydrogeology of a site influences the potential for on-site and off-site pollution as a result of development, and the extent of any pollution that may have occurred in thepast. Finally, competition between mineral extraction and other land uses is alsoan important topic in some circumstances (Ellison and Smith 1998).

5.3. Geomorphology

Geomorphology can be defined as "the study of land forms, and in particular their nature, origin, processes of development and material composition" (Cooke and Doornkamp 1990). 'Material composition' includes both the geology and, where present, the soil. Geomorphology therefore includes the study of topography(the terrain), the factors that have moulded the land to the present form (including the nature of the rock and soils in relation to the erosion and deposition caused by glaciers and rivers). Human impacts can include landscape/visual aspects, but also consequences such as erosion (Cooke and Doornkamp 1990), slope failure and subsidence, and sedimentation in aquatic systems. Some aspects of geomorphology, such as soil erosion, overlap with soilstudies.

5.4. Definitions and Concepts–Soils

The productive value of soils is determined by a number of important physical and chemical properties. An appreciation of a development's impacts on soils 202 Methods for environmental components requires an understanding of basic soil features. The coverage of soil science here is necessarily brief, and the reader is referred to Ashman and Puri (2002), Brady and Weil (2002), and Gerard (2000) for further information.

5.5.   Soil Composition

There are two major types of soil:mineral and organic. Typically mineral soils havefour major components: mineral particles, usually derived from weathering of parent rock (about 45 per cent of the volume); organic matter (about 5 per cent);water (about 25 per cent); and air (about 25 per cent). Organic matter is an important component of the soil that is derived mainly from decomposing vegetation. It combines with inorganic particles and cements like iron oxides and calcium carbonate to create stable structural aggregates. The nature of the organic matter in topsoils varies according to the vegetation cover and environmental conditions. In cool wet areas, the organic matter decomposes at a relatively slower rate and tends to be more acidic. In more temperate areas, the organic matter decomposes more completely to form stable complex compounds that are collectively known as humus. Most arable agricultural topsoils contain 2–6 percent organic matter, and structural stability is impaired at lower organic levels.

The inorganic component of soils consists of particles that are classified into standard size ranges (gravel, clay, silt and sand). There are a number of classifications of these particles, and the following is a simplified version from the British Standards Institution (BSI):

- Gravel – particle size over 2.0mm
- Sand – between 0.06 and 2.0mm
- Silt – between 0.002 and 0.06mm
- Clay – less than 0.002mm

These categories are known as separates, and their proportions in a soil defineits texture. Sandy soils contain at least 70 percent sand, and less than 15 percent clay; clays usually have no less than 40 percent clay; and loams have more equal proportions of clay, silt and sand. The texture of a soil is of great practical importance. Together with the humus content, it influences soil structure, which is the degree of aggregation of the separates, the size and shape of aggregates/structures, and both the range and total volume of pore spaces. Soil structure has a major influence on:

The soil's aeration properties:

- The capacity of the soil to retain moisture, and its hydraulic conductivity
- (and hence drainage properties); and

- The soil biota and plant root growth.

Texture also affects the behaviour of the soil at different moisture contents(its consistency). Thus clay soils tend to be less well drained than sandy and loamy soils. They may be water logged in winter, show poor infiltration and have a plastic consistency for much of the year. They are described as "heavy"as they are difficult to cultivate. Medium to heavy loams tend to have a morefriable consistency, and a greater capacity to make moisture available to plants during the summer. Sandy soils are described as "light". They are very friable and easy to work, but prone to drought. Loams are generally thought to have the most favourable textures for agriculture. Soil textures often vary with depth, as a result of the mixing and redistribution of parent materials during the Ice Ages, and subsequent soil-forming processes.

5.6.   The Soil Profile and Soil Classification

Clearly, it is important to know what type of soil is present in a study area. A pit dug into an undisturbed soil will reveal the topsoil and subsoil layers. Sucha vertical section is called a soil profile, and each individual layer is called a horizon. Two different soil profiles are shown in Fig. 5.1. Not all of the sub-soil horizons are always present, and the horizons are frequently subdivided. Pedological classifications of soils are concerned with natural horizons that have formed since the last Ice Age as a result of soil forming processes. Most natural soils have an organic-rich topsoil which contains humus. O and E horizons are eluvial upper horizons in which the inorganic particles have become depleted of nutrients as a result of the leaching effect of precipitation as it percolates through the profile to groundwater and water courses.

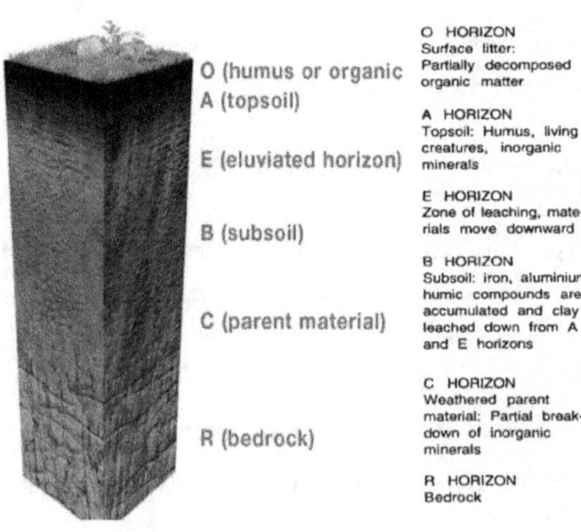

Fig. 5.1: Profile of a Typical Humus–iron Podzol

There are three superficial organic layers E, B and C which represent litter (leaves or needles), fermentation (where the breakdown of organic material contained in the litter largely occurs) and humus (where breakdown is largely complete). Beneath these are the eluvial O and E horizons (which are bleached and often grey in colour), illuvial B horizons (rich in iron), and the parent material of the C Horizon. These soils and their gleyed variants occur extensively over relatively cold and wet higher ground and some freely drained sandy parent materials in lowland areas. In these areas the main planning issues tend to be the protection of semi-natural habitats and wildlife conservation(redrawn from Bridges 1978).

In contrast, illuvial B horizons are often enriched with nutrients, iron, clays or organic matter which have been leached from above and deposited in the lower subsoils. The C horizon is the weathering parent material or rock.

The differentiation of horizons within the soil profile is the main criterion used in soil classifications. This chapter concentrates on the soils likely to be found, using the classification system adopted by Avery (1990).

Avery's terminology (or similar) is used in many British texts, and certainly seems to be the preferred terminology for British EIAs. There are, however, many other classifications, and two of these: the US Soil Taxonomy (USDA-NRCS 1999) which is used in American textbooks such as Brady and Weil (2002); and theWorld Reference Base for Soil Resources (WRB 2006) are gaining ground, evenin Britain. Table 5.1 compares the US terminology with the equivalent British terminology for major soils of the British Isles (Avery 1990). Many EU member states including Belgium, Eire, France, Germany, Italy the Netherlands and Portugal have their own distinctive soil classification systems, which in somecases contain elements of the USDA-NRCS and WRB classifications.

Table 5.1: A Comparison between the British Soil Classification of Avery (1990), and the USDA-NRCS (1999) Soil Taxonomy

Avery (1990)	USDA-NRCS	Notes
Podzols	Spodosols	Humid to per-humid temperate climates.Acidic soils characterised by grey coloured A and E horizons, and the deposition ofhumus and/or iron in the B horizon.
Brown soils	Mostly Alfisols	Humid temperate climates. Leached andelluviated soils, but reasonably fertile. Argillic B horizon. Includes Brown Earths.
Lithomorphic soils	Mostly Entisols	Thin (30cm) soils with no diagnostic subsurface horizon. Includes Rankers andRendzinas.
Gley soils	Aquic soils of a great variety of types	Soils characterised by saturation withwater for at least part of the time. Reducing conditions are prevalent.
Peat soils	Histosols	Organic soils, bog and fen peats, forming in humid climates often in depressions.
Man-made soils	Plaggepts and Arents	Ploughed and disturbed soils.

Almost all of the soils of the British Isles have been influenced by human activity to some extent. Avery (1990) restricts the term man-made soils tomineral soils where present or former management of the soil has resulted in distinctive features. Outside of the hills and uplands and smaller patches of low land heath (where the predominant soils are podzols which may be peaty and/or gleyed), most agricultural soils consist of gleyed brown earths, brown earths and gleys. They have topsoils that extend to relatively uniform depths over subsoils, with a gradual transition into the weathering parent material. Better quality soils tend to have loamy upper subsoils over lower subsoils that are generally heavier or lighter in texture, depending on the underlying parent material. Podzols (Fig.5.1) are typical of northern areas of Europe where they are associated with the boreal coniferous forest and heaths, and the climate is characteristically cold and wet. These soils are highly leached and acidic (pH often 3.0–4.5). They are little used for agriculture, but are very important for forestry and heathland habitats (including British lowland heaths), many of which areprotected by statutory designations. Podzols develop best on permeable sands and gravels.

Brown soils are generally associated with areas originally covered by deciduous forest and are the dominant soils of lowland Britain. There are many types of brown soil and Figure 5.2 shows one example, an acid brown soil. Brown earths are the best known and wide spread category of this group, and are fairly fertile,with pH 4.5–6.5. They are generally located in warmer and drier climates than podzols, and the precipitation/evapo transpiration ratio of the environments in which these soils develop is generally lower than that ofthe podzols. The amount of water percolating through the soil is sufficient tocause a moderate amount of leaching, but is not enough for podzol formation.

Most of the original forest that grew on brown soils has been cleared for agriculture.

In some places, the profiles have distinctive features that have been imposed by the underlying rock, or a geomorphological process. For example, Carboniferous limestone soils tend to have very shallow soil profiles over hard rock, and gravels form impenetrable layers or pans at a range of depths, often in alluvial areasor on plateau surfaces. Lithomorphic soils are thin soil types where the parentrock is the dominant feature in soil development, representing an early stage in soil development. The best-known lithomorphic soils are the rendzinas, which develop over chalk or limestone. In a typical rendzina, the A horizon, which isgenerally fairly thin, rests directly on the parent C horizon. The soil is very darkbrown or black in colour and is alkaline (pH 7.5–8.4). In contrast, rankers are young, acidic soils that develop over non-calcareous rocks such as sandstones.

In southern Britain, the climax vegetation on rendzinas is deciduous forest (e.g.beech, oak), but the trees has often cleared and these areas are now mostly used for agriculture. Gley soils are hydromorphic soils that are water logged for at least part of the year. Under these conditions, water saturates the soil, filling most of the porespaces and driving out air. Any remaining oxygen is soon used up by micro organisms, causing the development of anaerobic conditions in which the processof gleying (reduction of iron compounds from the ferric to the ferrous state) produces a distinctive blue-grey colouration.

Peat soils are a major soil type in some parts of the world, but cover a relatively minor fraction of the land surface of the UK (only 3 per cent of Englandand Wales, but rather more in Scotland and Ireland). Pure peat is partly decayed organic (mainly plant) material that accumulates where lack of oxygen, associated with water logging, in hibits the activity of microbial decomposer organisms. Mires (peatland ecosystems) occur where there is near-permanent.

Waterlogging and consequent peat accumulation. They provide valuable wildlife habitats, many of which are also protected by statutory designations. They are also important from a global warming perspective because they contain (and hence "lock up") a significant amount of carbon. Mires can be divided into bogsand fens, which differ largely in relation to their hydrology. According to MAFF (1988), peats contain at least 20 to 25 percent organic matter, depending on the clay content. The substratum of bogs is normally almost pure peat, but that in fens can contain high proportions of inorganic material such as marl (calcareous-clay mixtures). Similarly, while the peat in "active" bogsis normally saturated, many peatlands have fairly free drainage, at least near thesurface. However, lowering of water tables, e.g. by agricultural drainage schemes and/or water abstraction, can seriously damage peatland ecosystems and lead to soil loss by oxidation and erosion.

5.7.   Soil Structure

In most soils, the soil particles or separates are organized into aggregates. Soil structures called peds, vary in size and shape, and generally recognised standard types of structures are described in Hodgson (1997). Each soil horizon in a soiltype usually contains a type of texture and one shape and size of structure, but structure frequently varies with depth. For example, angular and mainly subangular blocky structures in loams become coarser (larger) with depth. In clays, there is frequently a transition from coarse angular and subangular blocky to prismatic structures with increasing depth. Sandy soils may have weakly developed angular and subangular structures in the upper subsoils, but sand particles lack cohesion, and such soils are usually devoid of structures (i.e. they are apedal) in the lower subsoil. In addition to drainage channels, soil structure provides airspaces, or pores within the aggregates or peds. These provide the space for plant roots, and the air and water necessary to sustain plants.

5.8. Soil Fertility

This is a vast topic and the reader is referred to Brady and Weil (2002), Cresser et al. (1993) and Troeh and Thompson (2005) for more details. Two major soil chemistry problems that are of importance in an EIA are low soil fertility, and toxicity, both of which will lead to poor plant growth. Low soil fertility is due either to low levels of nutrients (e.g. nitrogen, phosphorus, potassium and magnesium) in the soil, or their being made unavailable for plant uptake in someway. Soil toxicity is caused by high levels of toxic elements or compounds being present in the soil, usually as a result of human activity such as the spraying of pesticides, deposition of industrial waste, fuel spillage and the spreading of farm manure, slurries and sewage sludge. The source of toxic materials may not beon the affected land, and atmospheric deposition and movement in solution in groundwater may be significant. Some elements (e.g. copper and zinc) which are essential micronutrients for plant growth can be toxic at high concentrations.

Soil toxicity can be a significant limiting factor if levels permitted by the SoilCode (MAFF 1998) are exceeded. High levels of plant macronutrients, especially nitrogen and phosphorus, stimulateplant growth. However, the plant communities of semi-natural habitats,such as heathlands and "unimproved" grasslands, are adapted to low nutrient levels–and their value for biodiversity can be degraded by soil eutrophication that favours species such as vigorous grasses at the expense of ericoids and forbs. Soil pH per se rarely affects plant growth, but it strongly influences the availability of plant nutrients. Aluminium and nearly all of the heavy metals are much more available for plant uptake and entry to food chains in acid soils than in neutral or alkaline soils.

5.9. Land Evaluation

The pedological classification of soils considered above is based mainly on the nature of soil parent materials, modified by natural soil-forming processes. Land evaluation methodologies for the assessment of natural land quality (e.g.for agriculture or forestry) concentrate on the physical properties that cannot be altered by land management. For land use planning purposes, it has until recently been necessary to focus on determining the relative productive value of different areas of land for agriculture. The concept of sustainable development has introduced the need to protect the other functions of soils, which are valuablein respect of a wider range of environmental objectives.

Land quality (or capability) classification systems are based on the severity of climatic, topographic and soil limitations to the agricultural or silvicultural use of the land. Climatic limitations have an overriding down grading effect(irrespective of soil conditions) in areas that are cold and wet for most of the year (i.e. hills and uplands). In the more favourable locations (i.e. most of lowland Britain), soil wetness and liability to drought are the most common limiting factors. These are determined by both soil and climatic influences. The severity of a soil wetness limitation is determined by interactions between soil texture and structure, and the length of the period when soils are at field capacity inthe winter. The severity of a soil drought limitation is determined by interactions between soil texture and structure, and summer soil moisture deficits (SMDs) in relation to selected crops. Land quality is also determined by soil depth and stone content. Shallow and stony soils are downgraded, as are: sandy soils on sloping ground, which are prone to water erosion; and a relatively narrow range of fine sandy and silty soils, which are susceptible to wind erosion. Topographic limitations include steep slopes that preclude mechanised farm operations, andflood risk on river floodplains.

Soil Strategy and Soil Action Plan set out the Government's approach to the protection of different types of soil for a wide range of environmental functions, and not just the productive potential of the soil for agriculture and forestry. The main soil functions are:

- Soil and atmosphere interactions (e.g. the hydrological and carbon cycles);
- Food, timber and fibre production;
- Foundations for civil engineering;
- Supporting habitats and biodiversity;
- Providing raw materials (e.g. gravel); and
- Protecting archaeological features.

Conservation of soil potential without affecting soil nutrient as well as protect from surrounding contamination for sustainable soil management is very urgent need. The soil conservation practices giving to former are most effective to tool protect soil from the natural and anthropogenic activities.

BIBLIOGRAPHY

[1]   Abdallah S., Al-Zoubi., Abd El-Rahman A., Abueladas, Rami I. Al-Rzouq., Christian Camerlynck, Emad Akkawi, M. Ezarsky, Abu-Hamatteh, Z.S.H., Wasim Ali, and Samih Al Rawashdeh. (2007,3 94) American Journal of Environmental Sciences, 230-234.

[2]   Alan E. Musset, M. Aftab Khan. (2000). Looking into the earth: an introduction to geological geophysics. Cambridge University Press. pp. 1-12 & 181-183.

[3]   Anantharaman K.B., and Sethuraman S., (1984): geophysical exploration for uranium in suriyamalai batholiths, Salem district, Tamilnadu, india. Jour. Geol.Soc.India.

[4]   Antony Ravindran.A, Venkatesh.K and Essakiduarai. D (2012) Characterization of the geology and subsurface crystalline limestone mining using 2D ERI at Puthur Mines, Tirunelveli, Tamilnadu International Research Journal of Geology and Mining (IRJGM) (2276-6618) Vol. 2 (1) pp. 011-015.

[5]   Antony Ravindran.A., and Ramanujam (2012) A case study of crystalline limestone intrusion and fault zone identication using 2d eri technique in Ramco cements, pandalgudi mines, Tamilnadu, International Research Journal of Geology and Mining (IRJGM), pp. 011-015.

[6]   Asubiojo, O.I., P.O Aina and A.F. Oluwole (1991). Effect of cement production on the elemental composition of soil in the neighbouhood of two cement factories. Water Air Soil pollution.

[7]   Badmus B. S. and Olatinsu O. B. (2009) Geoelectric mapping and characterization of limestone deposits of Ewekoro formation, southwestern Nigeria , Journal of Geology and Mining Research Vol. 1(1) pp. 008-018.

[8]   Balint A, (1975). Ore sorting according to electrical conductivity: J. S. African Inst. Min. Metall., 40-44.

[9]   Barker, R.D., (1990) Environmental and groundwater applications", 2: 245 251.

[10]   Baynard, C.W. (2013). Remote sensing applications:Beyond land-use and land-cover change. Advances in Remote Sensing. Journal of Geomatics Vol 10 No. 2, 2016.

[11]   Dahlin T, Loke MH (1998). Resolution of 2D Wenner resistivity imaging as assessed by numericalmodelling, J. Appl. Geophysics, 38: 237- 249.

[12]   Dahlin,T., Loke, M.H.,(1998), Journal of Applied Geophysics, 38:.237-249.

[13]   Daniels F, Alberty RA (1966). Physical Chemistry.John Wiley and Sons, Inc.

[14]   E.Vasiliou and O.D. Mavrantza (2010). Using remote sensing to assess impact of mining activities on land and water resources. Mine Water Environment. Equbal, M.Z. and A.

Ambica (2012). Environmental impact assessment of Salem Chalk hills using remote sensing and GIS. International Journal of Computer Trends and Technology. Vol 3.

[15]   Edwards LS., (1977). A modified pseudosection for resistivity and IP. Geophysics, 42, 1020-1036.

[16]   Kerr T.L; O Sullivan P; Podmore D.C; Turner R; and Waters P (1994). Geophysics and iron ore exploration: examples from the Jimlebar and Shay Gap-Yarrie regions, Western Australia. "Proceedings of Exploration 97: Fourth Decennial International Conference on Mineral Exploration"edited by A.G. Gubins, 1997, 573–584.

[17]   Environmental Impact Assessment Proclamation (Proc. no. 299/2002), Addis Ababa, Ethiopia.

[18]   Fadele S.I., Jatau B.S. and Goki N.G (2013) "Subsurface structural characterization of filatan area a, zaria – kano road, using the 2d electrical resistivity tomography" Journal of Earth Sciences and Geotechnical engineering, vol. 3, no. 1, pp73-83.

[19]   Geological Survey of India.(1998). Geological and Mineral map of Tamilnadu and Pondicherry, Govt. of India.

[20]   Farmer, A.M. (1993). Effect of dust on vegetation - A review. Environmental pollution, 79, 63-75.

[21]   Geological Survey of India. (2006). Geology and Mineral Resources of the States of India: Part VI – Tamil Nadu and Pondicherry.

[22]   Geologists Association of Tamilnadu.(1984). Carbonate rocks, Tamilnadu.

[23]   Gleason, S., D. Faucette, M. Toyofuku, C.A. Torres and C.F. Bagley (2007). Assessing and mitigating the effects of wind blown soil on rare and common vegetation. Environmental Management, 40, 1016-1024.

[24]   Griffiths D.H. and Barker R.D., (1993) Journal of Applied Geophysics, ,29:211 – 226.

[25]   Howard L. Hartman, Jan M.Mutmansky. (2002). introductory mining engineering, 2nded,.John wiley& sons inc. pp. 47-81.

[26]   Iabal, M.F., M.R. Khan and A.H. Malik (2013). Land use change detection in the limestone exploitation area of Margalla Hills National Park (MHNP), Islamabad, Pakistan using geo-spatial techniques. Journal of Himalayan Earth Sciences.

[27]   Jhanwar, M.C. (1996). Application of remote sensing for environmental monitoring in Bijolia mining area of Rajasthan. Journal of Indian Society of Remote Sensing.

[28]   John Barnes, Richard J. Lisle. (2004) .Basic Geological Mapping, Fourth edition. John Wiley & Sons Ltd, England.

[29]   John M.Reynolds. (2011).An introduction to applied and environmental geophysics, 2nd ed. Wiley- Blackwell publication. pp. 1-18.

[30]   Jonathan E. Chambers, Oliver Kuras, Philip I. Meldrum, Richard D. Ogilvy, and Jonathan Hollands. (2006).Electrical resistivity tomography applied to geologic, hydrogeologic, and engineering investigations at a formerwaste-disposal site, Geophysics, vol. 71, no. 6 . P. B231–B239.

[31]   Jour. Marine Petrol. Geol. Odunuga, S. and G. Badru (2015). Landcover change, land surface temperature, surface albedo and topography in the Plateau Region of North-Central Nigeria. Land.

[32]   K.S. Subramanian and T.A. Selvan.(2001). Geology of Tamil Nadu and Pondicherry, Geol.Soc.India.

[33]   Kamila, A. and S. Chandra Pal (2015). Monitoring of land surface temperature and analyzing of environmental prediction on Asansol and Durgapur sub-division, Burdwan district, West Bengal using Landsat Imagery. International Journal of Remote Sensing & Geoscience.

[34]   Keller GV, Frischknecht FC, (1966). Electrical methods in geophysical prospecting, Pergamon Press Inc., Oxford.

[35]   Kelly SF (1962). Geophysical exploration for water by electrical resistivity.

[36]   Larcher, W. (1995). Physiological plant ecology: Ecophysiology and stress physiology of functional groups into plant morphology, physiology and pathology. Ph.D. Dissertation, University of California, Riverside.

[37]   Latifovic, R., K. Fytas, J. Chen and J. Paraszczak (2005). Assessing land cover change resulting from large surface mining development. International Journal of Applied Earth Observation and Geoinformation.

[38]   Leo T. armada , Carla B. Dimalanta , Graciano P. Yumul, Jr., and Rodolfo A. Tamayo, jr. (2009) "Georesistivity Signature of Crystalline Rocks in the Romblon Island Group, Philippines", Philippine journal of science 138 (2): 191-204.

[39]   Lines L.R; Treitel S, (1984) Tutorial: A review of least-squares inversion and its application to geophysical problems. Geophysical Prospecting, 32, 159-186.

[40]   Loke M.H, (2004). Tutorial: 2-D and 3-D Electrical Imaging Surveys. http://geoelectrical.com.

[41]   Loke M.H. and Barker R.D., (1996), Geophysical Prospecting, 44:131-152.

[42]   Loke M.H; Barker R.D, (1996).Rapid least-squares inversion of apparent resistivity pseudosections by a quasi-Newton method: Geophysical Prospecting, 44, 131-152.

[43]   Loke. M.H. (1997) Electrical imaging surveys for environmental and engineering studies – A practical guide to 2-D and 3-D surveys.info@terraplus.com.

[44]   M. Pichhode and K. Kumar Nikhil (2015). Effect of different mining dust on the vegetation of district Balaghat, M.P - A critical review. International Journal of Science and Research

[45]   Milsom , J. (1996). Field geophysics, 2nd ed. Wiley, New York.

[46]   Mock, J.F. and Bolton, P. (1993). The ICID Environmental Checklist to Identify Environmental Effects of Irrigation, Drainage and Flood Control Projects. HR Wallingford, Wallingford, UK

[47]   Mondal, S., J. Bandayopadhyay and D. Chakravarty (2014). Scientific investigation of the environmental impact of mines using geospatial techniques over a small part of Keonjhar district of Orissa. International Journal of Scientific and Research Publications.

[48]   Muawia A Dafalla1 and Fouzan A. AlFouzan. (2012) Influence of Physical Parameters and Soil Chemical Composition on Electrical Resistivity: A Guide for Geotechnical Soil Profiles, Int. J. Electrochem. Sci., 7 3191 – 3204.

[49]   Nagendra, R., B.V. Kamalakkannan, Gargi Sen, Harry Gilbert, D. Bakkiaraj, A. Nallapa Reddy and B.C. Jaiprakash (2011). Sequence surfaces and paleobathymetric trends in Albian to Maastrichtian sediments of Ariyalur area, Cauvery Basin, India.

[50]   Nair, E.M. (1974). Carbonates in the Cauvery basin, South india, Carbonate rocks of Tamil Nadu, Geologist's Association of Tamil Nadu, Madras.

[51]   Nathan. N.P., Krishna Rao, A.V., Bhalla, J.K., Balasubramanian, E., Subramanian, N., Oberoi, L.K., Natarajan, V., Gopalakrishnan, K., and Raman. R. (1990) : Geochemistry and Geochronology of the pegmatoidal granite of New England water assn., 76: 118-189.

[52]   Orowe M. O.K., V. S. Singh, V. AnandRao and RatnakarDhakate,(2008), Current science, 95(8):1067-1071.

[53]   Osazuwa.B, and Chiichii. E (2010) "Two-dimensional electrical resistivity survey around the periphery of an artificial lake in the Precambrian basement complex of northern Nigeria1,department of physics, ahmadu bello university, zaria, kaduna state, nigeria." International journal of physical sciences vol. 5(3), pp. 238-245.

[54]   Philip Kearey, Michael Brooks, Ian Hill. (2002). An Introduction Geophysical Exploration, third edition, Blackwell Science Ltd. Pp: 1-6.

[55]   PK. Banerjee, S. Ghosh. (1997). Elements of prospecting for non-fuel mineral deposits. Allied publishers ltd. Pp. 210-276.

[56]   Ranade, P. (2007). Environmental impact assessment of land use planning around the leased limestone mine using remote sensing techniques, Iran.   Journal of Health. Science Engineering.

[57]   Rathore, C.S. and R. Wright (1993). Monitoring environmental impacts of surface coal mining. International Journal of Remote Sensing, 14, 1021– 1042.

[58]   S.I. Fadele, B.S. Jatau and N.G. Goki. (2013). Subsurface Structural Characterization of Filatan Area A, Zaria–Kano Road, using the 2D ElectricalResistivity Tomography, Journal of Earth Sciences and Geotechnical Engineering, vol. 3, no. 1, 73-83.

[59]   Sankari-Trichengode area, Salem District, Tamilnadu.Indian Minerals.Vol.48 (1&2), pp.113-122, 1994.

[60]   Sobrino, J.A., Z.L. Li, G. Soria and J.C. Jiménez (2003). Land surface temperature and emissivity retrieval from remote sensing data, Recent Res. Dev. Geophys. 4, 21–44.

[61]   Srinivasamoorthy K, Sarma VS, Vasantavigar M, Vijayaraghavan K, Chidambaram S and Rajivganthi R (2009).Electrical imaging techniques for groundwater pollution studies: A case study from Tamilnadu state, South India, Earth Sci. Res. J. Vol. 13, No. 1 30-39.

[62]   Stefouli, M. and P. Tsombos (1998). Identification and monitoring of surface mining and smelter pollution using remote sensing techniques: A case study in Lavreotiki Peninsula, Attiki prefecture, Greece. Proceedings of the colloquium space techniques for environmental management in the mediterranean region, 176– 282.

[63]   Turner, G.F. (2012). The potential impacts of dust loading on vegetation surrounding mine sites. 5th Environmental Management in Mining WA, Perth,

[64]   Woldai, T. (2001). Application of remotely sensed data and GIS in assessing the impact of mining activities on the environment. 17th International Mining Congress and Exhibition of Turkey.

[65]   World Bank (1991) Environmental Assessment Sourcebook, Volume 1. World Bank Technical Paper No. 139. World Bank, Washigton D.C.

[66]   World Bank (1993) Environmental Screening, Environmental Assessment Sourcebook Update No. 2, Environmental Department, The world Bank, Washinton D.C.

[67]   World Bank (1996) Analysis of alternatives in Environemtal Assessment. Environmental Assessment Sourcebook Update No. 17, Environmental Department, world Bank, Washinton D.C.

www.ingramcontent.com/pod-product-compliance
Lightning Source LLC
Chambersburg PA
CBHW071154130726
47998CB00002B/510